Anna Mancini

Your Dreams Can Save Your Life

How and why your dreams warn you of every danger: earthquakes, tidal waves, tornadoes, storms, landslides, plane crashes, assaults, attacks, burglaries, etc.

Buenos Books America
www.buenosbooks.us

Publisher: Buenos Books America,
http://www.buenosbooks.us
order@buenosbooks.us

ISBN: 978-1-932848-91-5 (Printed version)
ISBN: 978-1-932848-88-5 (E-Book)

First published in French by Buenos Books International, in June 2012 (Original title: Vos Rêves Peuvent Vous Sauver la Vie)

ABOUT THE AUTHOR

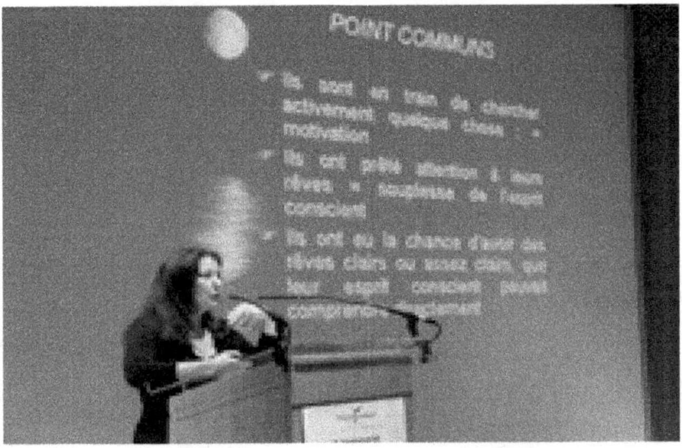

Anna Mancini, a French woman of Italian origin, lives in Paris and is a writer, tutor and lecturer. Inspired by her family culture, she has been interested in dreams from a young age.

Later, while she was writing her PhD thesis on patent law, a great dream changed her life. This special and very clear dream gave her the solution to a mystery of ancient Roman law[1] that many researchers all over the world had not managed to solve.

Against all expectation, instead of being welcomed with enthusiasm by the academic world, this discovery, whose oneiric origin she did not mention, caused her to be excluded from the university and blocked by her thesis supervisor in her career as a lawyer. This is why she then chose to dedicate herself entirely to research and experimentation concerning the oneiric process.

For many years she has observed dreams and also dreamers, and has done experiments in order to understand what influence their environment and lifestyle have on the content of their dreams. For her research, she has also made use of old unknown teachings on the human psyche that have survived through the remains of old judicial systems.

Thanks to this original method of working on dreams and with the help of her own dreams that have guided her throughout her research, she has been able to:

---

[1] *Ancient Roman Solutions to Modern Legal Issues*, Buenos Books America, www.buenosbooks.us

- develop an innovative and efficient method for the interpretation of oneiric language;
- develop a technique that allows us to ask our subconscious questions and receive answers, whatever the subject area;
- understand which conditions are favourable and unfavourable for creative dreams;
- and discover many other things that make our waking life easier and increase the vitality of dreamers.

She created the research organisation 'Innovative You' in 1995, based in Paris, within which she has been able with others to experiment with the techniques for working on dreams that she has developed after long personal research.

Anna Mancini has written many books; a list can be found on her website:

www.amancini.com

She runs workshops, gives lectures and coaches people so that they too can use their dreams to improve all aspects of their lives and also become more creative. She teaches these oneiric creativity techniques in France and abroad, in particular in the research and innovation departments of companies.

If you wish to be coached, arrange a lecture, a workshop or a course on dreams, please contact the author:

info@amancini.com

Anna Mancini's lectures, workshops and courses are regularly announced on the blog section of her personal website which you can subscribe to.

CONTENT

INTRODUCTION

In recent times throughout the world we have witnessed an acceleration in the rhythm of natural disasters. Despite advances in technology, authorities are not always able to warn populations in time. Because of this humanity continues to pay a heavy price for nature's fury in terms of human lives and material damage.

However, this situation could easily be improved. Many lives could be saved and considerable damage avoided, if everyone learned to listen better to the messages that their body - which is always in communication with Nature- sends to them through the channel of dreams. Indeed, there is no more efficient instrument than living matter, (for example the body of a person or an animal) for detecting early warning signs of natural disasters and for making an escape possible, before it is too late. This ability that the human or animal body has to perceive changes in its environment, is part of instinct.

Earth, just like ourselves, is not only matter, it is also energy, and its physical transformations which sometimes take us unawares by their apparent suddenness are in reality preceded well before the outbreak of the natural elements, by earthly and cosmic energy and vibratory changes. These are changes that the human body today is still capable of sensing without us being aware of it, and it is also this natural phenomenon that allows animals, in the event of natural disasters, to survive better than most humans who have lost their intuition, who no longer know how to communicate with their bodies and no longer pay attention to their dreams.

Our body is extraordinarily sensitive to the slightest changes in our environment. It also has a powerful instinct that warns it when it senses a danger and sounds the alarm through the channel of dreams or intuition. It possesses a remarkable sensitivity to energy changes and other early warning signs of natural disasters. Careful observation over quite a long period of time of the links between dreams and reality reveals that our body is also very sensitive to the thoughts and emotions of other human beings. Indeed, they also have an energy dimension, sometimes clearly and directly perceptible to some people in a waking state.

My years of research away from the mainstream, on the links between dreams, reality and people's environment, have allowed me to understand how the human body as a whole receives a lot of information from its environment, and how this information which no longer surfaces on modern man's consciousness in a waking state is nevertheless transmitted to the brain through dreams. Thanks to my research I have developed a method that is both original and very simple that enables nearly everyone to use the ability to dream in order to improve many aspects of their waking life. These include becoming more able to perceive dangers that threaten us, whether they be natural, human or technological.[2]

My way of using the ability to dream is different to all the methods that exist currently in literature on dreams, whether it be scientific, psychoanalytic, shamanic, etc. It is pragmatic, based on more than twenty years of objective observations and everyone can use it, with a little bit of time each morning and some basic personal hygiene and psychological health rules.

By reading this book, you too could learn to develop your ability to sense any kind of danger that might threaten you, in order to avoid it, or even in some circumstances to save your life and that of loved ones.

For example you will be better able to:

- avoid accidental death by escaping before the start of a natural disaster: earthquake, volcanic

---

[2] We can also do many other things with our dreams, for example develop our creativity or manage our health better, as I explain in my book *The meaning of dreams* and in my seminars and training.

eruption, land slide, flood, storm, tidal wave, and avalanche;

- frustrate the plans of attackers, terrorists, thieves, rapists or burglars;
- know, before going off on a trip, for example by plane or boat, if you are going to arrive safe and sound at your destination;
- sense many other traps and dangers.

By using the technique which is available to all, which I explain in this book, you will learn to 'retrieve' the important information which is available to you when you are dreaming. The most gifted will also be able to develop a greater sensitivity and intuition upon waking, which will enable you to react even more effectively to the dangers of your environment.

Before explaining to you how you can use your dreams in order to protect yourself from the dangers of your environment, in the first chapter I would like to speak to you about animals which have been able to keep their conscious sensitivity to their environment. It is thanks to this corporal and psychological sensitivity upon waking, that animals are able to flee, sometimes long before the start of disasters, whilst most human beings, taken by surprise, lose their lives in these same circumstances.

In the second chapter, I would like to talk to you about some famous people, who in the past have benefited naturally from their dreams by being warned of dangers, without, however, having always taken advantage of them to avoid dangers. In a third chapter I will explain a method to you that will allow you to safely and easily develop your oneiric and intuitive abilities by yourself.

Finally I will end by talking to you about dreams giving false warnings of disasters, in other words nightmares and their causes. I will explain to you how and why some nightmares happen and how it is possible to avoid them.

CHAPTER 1:

ANIMALS THAT FLEE BEFORE NATURAL DISASTERS

While human beings continue to go about their daily business, not sensing anything coming until the last minute; it has often been observed that wild animals flee to protect themselves before the onset of natural disasters, while domestic animals show unusual behaviour and also flee if they are allowed to.

For example, after the earthquake in China in Tangshan on the 28th July 1976, which killed 240, 000 people, survivors confirmed that they had noticed unusual behaviour in wild and domestic animals sometime before the start of the earthquake: dogs barking, agitated behaviour in snakes and mice, abnormal behaviour in cows and horses, etc. They then learned from the experience and strongly advised paying attention to unusual behaviour coming from animals.

Sadly later, again in China, despite the roads being filled with thousands of amphibians, which were fleeing an earthquake several days before its start, the population of Sichuan went calmly about its daily business, unlike the frogs and toads automatically seeking refuge, as far away as possible from the place where a terrible earthquake happened on the 12th May 2008, which killed 80,000 people. This exodus of amphibians was so spectacular that photographs were posted on the Internet. In some of them we can see people who are probably dead today, cycling calmly along roads that are full of thousands of frogs.[3] This phenomenon involving frogs was also observed in Italy when an earthquake struck Rome on the 6th April 2009[4] and in many other circumstances which have been widely reported on the Internet.[5]

Other animals have also demonstrated their ability to sense imminent danger when natural disasters threaten. For example in Sri Lanka after the terrible tsunami which destroyed the Yala national park on the 26th December 2004, no elephants were killed. This tsunami resulted in 300,000 people losing their lives or going missing in Thailand, South India, the Maldives, the Seychelles, Mauritius, Madagascar and the east coast of Africa, and despite this the Sri Lankan authorities claimed that they had not found any

---

[3] http://heavenawaits.wordpress.com/frogs-predicting-earthquakes/

[4]http://www.allvoices.com/contributed-news/5542154-is-frog-species-have-earthquake-forecast

[5] Earthquake in Aquila, Italy
http://www.guardian.co.uk/science/2010/mar/31/toads-detect-earthquakes-study

dead elephants. These animals as well as other wild animals in the park sought shelter before the outbreak of severe weather.[6]

In Martinique in 1902, the eruption of Mount Pelée killed 300,000 inhabitants of Saint-Pierre, but the wild animals fled and survived having sensed the imminent eruption.

Learning of these few examples, which were chosen amongst many others, we cannot help but be struck:

- by the fact that animals have retained this natural, very practical ability to sense danger consciously, sometimes several days before the outbreak of the elements.
- by the fact that in the same circumstances almost all human beings did not sense anything coming.

We might be tempted to conclude, like so many other researchers, that animals have clearly superior faculties to those of human beings in terms of being able to detect the dangers in their environment. However, as we will see, this is not the case. Indeed, if human beings bothered to use

---

[6] http://weblog.sinteur.com/2004/12/tsunami-kills-few-animals-in-sri-lanka

their natural abilities, they would far surpass all the animals on the planet.

It is through twenty years of observation of the links between dreams and reality in many people, that I have been able to notice that human beings have even more sophisticated abilities than those of animals in terms of safeguarding themselves from any kind of danger; and not only natural dangers.

But I am not the only person, far from it, to have noticed that human beings are capable of sensing the dangers of their environment more precisely than animals. There are many historical accounts of such abilities throughout history. Some of these accounts often concern people who having been warned of dangers thanks to dreams, were able or unable to escape them in reality, depending on the decisions that they took following their warning dream. Other accounts concern people who had the ability upon waking to sense disturbances in nature. I am now going to talk to you in the chapter that follows about some of the most striking examples, chosen among so many others.

CHAPTER 2:

HISTORICAL EXAMPLES OF PEOPLE WHO RETAINED THEIR ABILITY TO SENSE THE DANGERS OF THEIR ENVIRONMENT

Throughout history there have been human beings who have been able to sense the dangers of their environment, either upon waking or while sleeping. Goethe was capable of sensing earthquakes that happened a long distance away, while the infamous Adolph Hitler was saved thanks to a dream.

Johann Peter Eckermann who was Goethe's secretary during the last nine years of his life, wrote a work entitled: *Conversations with Goethe*.[7] In this book Eckermann recounts the fact that upon waking Goethe was capable of sensing earthquakes which had taken place a long distance away.[8]

---

[7] Original German title: *Gespräche mit Goethe*

[8] There are other examples on the following website: http://www.answers.com/topic/earthquake-prediction#ixzz1oYvA9qYs

One November night in 1917 during the Battle of the Somme, Adolph Hitler, who was then only a young corporal, woke up scared by a terrible nightmare. He had dreamt that he was dying, covered with building rubble. In order to calm himself he went outside the building he was sleeping in with his regimental comrades, in order to take some air, while telling himself happily that it was just a nightmare. However, some moments later a bomb fell on the building which he had just left and killed all the other soldiers who were sleeping there.[9]

In the case of Adolph Hitler, given the figure, it would surprise me greatly if he had in this case benefited from divine intervention. He simply and naturally sensed a danger that threatened him thanks to his subconscious. He was obviously more perceptive than all his unfortunate regimental comrades and was better able to communicate with his subconscious and body and had a better survival instinct. I would like to add that it is often the case that people who are normally very rational, who rarely dream and do not pay any attention to their dreams, suddenly are superstitious or believe in divine intervention when they have been saved from danger thanks to a dream occurring naturally. Although in some cases the possibility of supernatural intervention

---

[9] *Your dreams and what they mean*, Nerys Dee, p. 28

cannot be totally ruled out, most of the time dreaming about a danger that threatens us is a natural phenomenon, which is wholly explainable and linked to our subconscious ability to perceive the dangers in our environment, in order to protect ourselves.

Further back in history in Roman times, we can find an account of the warning dream of Calpurnia, the wife of Julius Caesar. Calpurnia was Julius Caesar's last wife until his death in 44 BC. One night she dreamt that her husband was being assassinated at the Senate and she warned him, imploring him to protect himself. Caesar did not listen to her; he went as usual to the Senate, where he was indeed assassinated.[10]

In this example we see that Caesar, who was directly affected by the danger, had not dreamed of it himself and that he did not seem to give dreams any importance, at least not those of his wife. And yet, when we live as a couple or as a family it is often the case that we have dreams which contain information about other members of the family. I will talk again later about this natural phenomenon and the reasons for which it happens. I am now going to mention another famous historical example, that of a former president of the United States.

---

[10] http://fr.wikipedia.org/wiki/Calpurnia_Pisonis

In the United States, twelve days before his assassination, President Abraham Lincoln had a dream that made such an impression on him that he had to talk about it with his nearest and dearest. Amongst them was Ward Hill Lamon who recounted the dream that Abraham Lincoln had then told him, in this extract from a work entitled: *Memories of Abraham Lincoln 1847-1865.*[11]

"*About ten days ago, I retired very late. I had been up waiting for important dispatches from the front. I could not have been long in bed when I fell into a slumber, for I was weary. I soon began to dream. There seemed to be a death-like stillness about me. Then I heard subdued sobs, as if a number of people were weeping. I thought I left my bed and wandered downstairs. There the silence was broken by the same pitiful sobbing, but the mourners were invisible. I went from room to room; no living person was in sight, but the same mournful sounds of distress met me as I passed along. I saw light in all the rooms; every object was familiar to me; but where were all the people who were grieving as if their hearts would break? I was puzzled and alarmed. What could be the meaning of all this? Determined to find the cause of a state of things so mysterious and so shocking, I kept on until I arrived at the East Room, which I*

---

11 *Histoires Paranormales du Titanic*, Bertrand Méheust, J'ai lu, 2006

entered. There I met with a sickening surprise. Before me was a catafalque, on which rested a corpse wrapped in funeral vestments. Around it were stationed soldiers who were acting as guards; and there was a throng of people, gazing mournfully upon the corpse, whose face was covered, others weeping pitifully. 'Who is dead in the White House?' I demanded of one of the soldiers, 'The President,' was his answer; 'he was killed by an assassin.' Then came a loud burst of grief from the crowd, which woke me from my dream. I slept no more that night; and although it was only a dream, I have been strangely annoyed by it ever since."

Three days later, when he was in the theatre with his wife, President Abraham Lincoln was assassinated in his presidential box by an actor and political opponent.

The sinking of the Titanic on the 14th April 1912 was -according to the investigation lead by Ian Stephenson- foreseen in a dream by some of the passengers who duly cancelled their trip.[12]

---

[12] *The New World of Dreams, Woods And Greenhouse*, p. 86; See also: http://www.metapsychique.org/Prevision-de-desastres.html;

On the 21st October 1966 in Aberfan, a small English mining village, a school was buried under a landslide of 500 tonnes of mining debris killing 144 people, mainly children. Amongst them was Eryl Mai Jones, aged 10 years, who had dreamed of the event two weeks before it happened. She had said to her mother that she was not scared of dying, because she would die in the company of her class mates Peter and June. On the morning of the 20th October she spoke to her mother about a dream that she had just had in these words: "Mummy, I want to talk to you about a dream that I had last night. I dreamt that I was going to school and there was no school anymore. Something black had covered it."[13]

If this child had been my daughter I would have tried to understand more about this from the first dream, I would have studied the dreams of the other children in her school and I myself would have definitely dreamt of the coming event and tried to do something to save the lives of all these children.

In reading these few examples, it is easy to understand that, thanks to their dreams, some human beings are even more able than animals to perceive the risks of their environment, be they

---

[13] See also the article published in the British Journal of the Society for Psychic Research (vol. 44), 1967

natural or not. It therefore begs the question, why don't governments create organisations for recording disaster dreams in order to help the general population?

As we will see, such organisations were indeed created, but these initiatives ended due to a failure that will be explained in the light of our own research into the connections between dreams and waking life and dreamers' physical and energetic environment.

CHAPTER 3:

THE FAILURE OF 'DREAM RECORDING BUREAUX' AND THE REASONS WHY

An English psychiatrist, Dr Barker, was so struck by the events in Aberfan that he decided to create the *British Premonition Bureau* in January 1967. He thought that through this bureau it would be possible to warn populations and save lives. Following this, a year later the Americans in turn created, in New York, the *Central Premonition Bureau*. A bureau was also created in Belgium.

Unfortunately, we know from the press of the time that the English and American experiments were inconclusive. Firstly the bureaux received many dreams of natural disasters that never happened and which were ultimately only 'false warnings'. Secondly they recorded only a small number of dreams which turned out to be premonitions.

Due to a lack of effectiveness the two bureaux decided to end their operations. However a change in their operating procedure would have allowed them to achieve the objectives that they had set out to achieve.

The fact that these bureaux received mainly false warnings is not surprising given that anyone, whether or not they knew their 'oneiric landscape', whether or not they had completed work in order to understand their dreams could send their dreams, or rather nightmares! And yet to know whether a dream is really a warning, it is not enough to take note of the dream and record it. A lot of additional information is also necessary concerning the diurnal life of the dreamer who has sent in the dream, his physical and mental health, his activities on the day or days preceding the dream, what he or she has consumed, what he watched on the television or in the cinema, where he slept, whether he is calm or stressed, and other information which I will talk to you further about, giving examples of false warnings and their causes linked to the dreamer's way of life.

All this information is clearly very personal and no nation would like a public or private organisation to be able to interfere to this degree in their private lives, even for a good cause. So what should be done?

In general it would be wiser for all individuals to learn how to use their dreams entirely by themselves and also, for one or more 'dream observation' organisations to be created, gathering together skilled and trained dreamers. Ideally everyone should learn how to retrieve useful information from dreams and how to better dream.

We should all know perfectly well our 'oneiric landscape' in order to be able to distinguish between true warning dreams and simple nightmares.

It would be good if public organisations gathering together very gifted people in this area could be created all over the world and if they could work together. But the best way of protecting yourself from dangers on a personal level (and also in order to be able to warn your loved ones) requires personal development, seeing as this is available to almost everyone, with it you do a bit of homework each morning for about a year and have a good lifestyle. By developing our own natural ability to perceive dangers, we shield ourselves from regular anxiety caused by people who announce – in good or bad faith – terrible calamities that are imminent, or even the end of the world!

This personal work consists in observing your dreams and reality in a certain way and in doing some small experiments in order to be able to understand better how the body communicates with the brain and vice-versa.

By keeping a notebook of dreams and reality in the manner explained later, you will be able to understand how your body works on an informational level. Thanks to this understanding you will be able to benefit from your dreams by being warned in time, sometimes long in advance, of the dangers that threaten you.

In the chapter that follows I will explain to you how the human body works at the point where the visible and the invisible meet and how it is possible to use this ability in order to 'recover' as much information as possible relating to your survival in an environment (natural, technological or human) which may become hostile.

CHAPTER 4:

THE INFORMATIONAL PROCESSING OF THE HUMAN BODY AT THE POINT WHERE DREAMS AND REALITY MEET

What I am going to explain here comes from my personal research over a very long period. It will help you, I hope, to understand how your body works at the point where dreams and reality meet, the visible and invisible and to learn to take more advantage of this phenomenon.

Although in the Western world we are mainly interested in the material aspect of existence, our body is nonetheless material and immaterial at the same time. In other words, we all have an aspect that is both corporeal/material and energetic/informational. In terms of the informational field, our body is simultaneously a transmitter, receiver and a transformer of energy/information.

Most of the informational, corporeal activities happen without us being conscious of them. Thanks to its sensitivity to energy, vibrations and to the intangible information of its immediate or wider environment, the body is far more able than the mind of sensing changes in its environment and in sensing information, energy, emotions or thoughts of other living beings.

On an informational level each living being is surrounded by a bubble of energy/information in which the information emitted in the environment and information from the environment circulates. This process is like an uninterrupted breath, both upon waking and during sleep.

In a waking state, modern man's conscious mind is most often disconnected from corporeal feeling and therefore does not benefit from useful information that his body could give him if he had kept in contact with it, like wild animals. During dreams, in most cases the mind does not play a dominant role, therefore it is a good time for the body to pass information to the sleeper that could not reach him in a waking state. This information may concern the energy quality of his environment, but also people encountered in the course of the previous day.

Indeed, when people meet, even if they do not touch, their bodies exchange all kinds of information via their "informational bubbles".[14] We scan each other from the first contact and in

---

[14] According to the various spiritual traditions who have also observed this phenomenon, we could also say: through their auras, or through their subtle or etheric body, etc. However, non-religious vocabulary is preferred in this book, so that this book can be used by everyone, believers and non-believers.

our subconscious we garner all kinds of information about the people we speak to (their vital energy level, their life story, where they come from, their emotional state, their health, their recent and distant past, their genetic heritage, etc.) while our mind occupies itself most of the time solely with what the person is saying, their appearance, clothes and social status! Some information gathered by the body will reach the conscience through dreams, but they might sometimes be very distorted or symbolic and therefore incomprehensible to people who are not familiar with the language of dreams, which is also very largely that of nature.

When we enter a place, wherever that may be, while our mind sees with the eyes, listens with the ears and smells with the nose, our body senses via the soles of the feet, the palms of the hands and the whole surface of the skin, the energy and vibrations of places. All this information collected by the body[15] is felt to a varying extent depending

---

[15] Some spiritual traditions teach that the human body receives information through its aura or etheric body. This phenomenon gives the sense of having like a second skin at a distance varying from several centimetres to several metres depending on the person. Then the information needs to pass through the body so that it can surface on diurnal consciousness thanks

on the individual, as a place's atmosphere. Are you capable of sensing the difference between the energy atmosphere of a church, a bar, a sunny beach, a forest in the spring, a cemetery or a hospital? Or are you one of those people who are controlled by their mind, who no longer have the instinct to leave some places (rooms, restaurants, shops, the areas around abattoirs, etc.) which are materially beautiful but energetically harmful, because they no longer feel the energetic harmfulness of some places on a conscious level and allow themselves to be seduced by an apparent material harmony? Whether you belong to the first or second group of people, you would all benefit from developing your ability to communicate with your body. It is very easy to do; all it requires is to observe for a period of time the links between your dreams and your reality by applying the method that I am now going to explain to you.

---

to the brain, through the channel of dreams and intuition.

CHAPTER 5:

HOW TO DEVELOP YOUR PERCEPTIONS BY USING YOUR DREAMS

Here I will explain quickly how to proceed. This book is perfectly suitable to enable you to carry out your own experiments and develop your ability to sense the dangers in your environment, whatever they may be. If you want to know more or go further you can also read my work *The meaning of dreams*[16] which will give you more detailed information and will also explain to you many other things that it is possible to do with dreams.

In the morning, in a waking state, do not turn on the radio, do not dash to your computer, do not think about your daily activities. Remain a while in bed; try to remember your dreams. If nothing comes, change position in bed, then sit down and try again to remember your dreams. By doing this you will find that your ability to remember your

---

[16] *The Meaning of Dreams*, Anna Mancini, Buenos Books International, Paris (This is the second edition of *The Intelligence of Dreams*). This work has also been translated into Italian and Spanish.

dreams will gradually improve. Very often all it takes is to pay attention to dreams, for your ability to dream and remember them to develop. If at the start you do not manage to remember your dreams, then write down in a notebook (or any other thing you prefer: voice recorder, iPad, computer, etc.) your state of mind and your physical state in a waking state, also the thoughts that are running through your mind. They could sometimes be songs. Record all this and also note down your reality in general as I later explain.

Most people who say they do not remember their dreams are people who do not sleep enough. Often all it takes is for them to have a lie in for their 'dream machine' to be put back on track. If it is not lack of sleep that is the problem, it is necessary to apply some of the techniques found at the back of the book in the 'Replies to frequent questions' section, in order to recover and develop memory of dreams.

I really like to train difficult cases and see how these people's lives change for the better, in many aspects, when they regain access to information from their dreams.

When you remember your dreams it is necessary to note them down in as much detail as possible, as if you were talking about a film that you are watching. As well as the story, if there is one, note down your feelings and where objects, animals and other people are situated in space and in relation to you. Note down everything that you felt 'bodily' during the dream, sounds, smells, feelings of happiness or unhappiness, the intensity of the colours, etc. Note down the colours of the clothes of the people are wearing in your dreams, the quality of the animal's fur, the colour of their eyes etc.

Concerning reality you can be a lot briefer. All it takes is to note down in broad detail what you did yesterday, to make a note of the people that you met, what you read, watched on television, browsed on the internet, listened to on the radio, etc. Also note down what you ate, the places where you went, the place where you slept (if it wasn't your normal bedroom), the person you slept next to and if you had sex and with whom. Note down the day's mood (excellent, good, bad), your physical health (great shape, tired, pains, illness, well-being). Did you have any discomfort, a cold, heaviness in your legs, problems with physical health? Did you feel happy, depressed, nervous, etc? Note all this down. Also note down any other information that you judge to be useful in relation to your activities, your current projects or your emotional life.

Perhaps it surprises you that I advise taking notes on your sexual relations? You will see by doing your own observational work on the links between dreams and your reality that when we have sex, on an invisible level important things happen of which we are not often aware: we exchange our energy, the vibrations of our past, our energy environment and we keep all of this in our own 'system' for a while, before releasing a large amount of it. Therefore when we have sexual relations with someone new, our dreams are consequently transformed and we can dream of information that in reality relates to our partner. There would be a lot to write on this subject! It is up to you to observe what happens, and to draw lessons from this for your love life.

Concerning dreams, do not hesitate to note down everything you remember, and even information that disturbs you, that seems unimportant or even stupid to you. Work with as much neutrality as possible, without judging, with honesty, as if you were describing a film. Above all allow your thoughts, ideas and feelings to happen freely. Do not judge, do not pay any attention to style or spelling. What's more, spelling mistakes can be the key to interpreting the dream. Even if you believe you do not 'know how to write' do not worry about this. This is not important in relation to your objective and when you note down your dreams and your reality, do this freely, without censorship.

When you begin your work of noting things down, do not attempt to understand your dreams. At this stage it is not useful and you will be able to do it much more effectively and ably after some time spent noting down your dreams and reality. Indeed, when you have gathered enough material, all it will take is to re-read your notebook in one go and you will see the connections between your dreams and your reality. In other words you will see that the same oneiric symbol appears simultaneously with a similar kind of situation experienced in reality. This simultaneity will allow you to decipher precisely the meaning of your oneiric symbolism. I explain this more in detail at the end of this work in the 'Replies to frequent questions' section where I give you advice for interpreting your dreams through the method of observing the connections between your dreams and reality.

It is important to become familiar with the language of your dreams and to understand your own oneiric code because sometimes dreams which warn you of dangers can be symbolic and in this case it is necessary to know how to interpret them.

For example, one of my friends who is self-employed told me a dream that had really affected him in which he saw his closest colleague who had been working for him for several years stealing from the till. This dream was so strong and had seemed so real that despite the trust he had in his colleague who had been working with him for several years, he had checked the till but had not found anything amiss. He then thought that his dream was false, but it turned out that it was simply symbolic. Indeed, he learnt a little bit later through his clients that his closest colleague was causing his clientele to stay away by sabotaging the reputation of her boss. This is what had been presented in my friend's dream as 'stealing from the till'. This friend could have straightaway understood the dream and reacted more quickly if he had kept a notebook of dreams and reality. However, this was not the case.

This example explains the interest in understanding symbolic dreams. But one should be patient and not rush things. For our objective (the development of the ability to sense danger) the most important thing initially is to train the conscious, subconscious and the body to communicate better. Understanding of the meaning of your dreams will simply happen by itself once your body, subconscious and conscious have re-established the connections that modern life has severed in most of us.

Therefore, initially, do no try to understand your dreams with your mind. Instead, every morning allow the information, atmosphere, images and colours of your dreams to come to the surface of your conscious without judging them. Accept them, experience them in a state of meditation. You will find that sometimes, as soon as you start to write down the snippets of the dream that you remember, other whole dreams will suddenly come to mind. In the morning you must leave a little bit of time for yourself, to relax and immerse yourself in your interior being instead of thinking about all your daily tasks.

By doing such a simple thing for some time you will improve communication between your conscious, subconscious and your body and little by little you will regain the optimal conditions for being warned of possible dangers in your immediate environment (and in some circumstances even further afield). Modern life has little by little cut us off from our bodily feeling, our interior life and nature, mainly because the mind and our daily activities in increasingly artificial environments have taken precedence. But nothing stops us from learning again to take advantage of the ability we all have in a latent state and which today mainly manifests itself through dreams.

By re-establishing contact with your interior life, subconscious and with nature through your body, just like animals you will be better able to sense what happens in your energy environment and you will also be able to seek shelter before the start of events such as: earthquakes, tidal waves, tornadoes, avalanches, volcanic eruptions, etc. You will be able to go further than animals and know, for example, if there are technical faults in a nearby nuclear power station, or in a plane, car or boat in which you are intending to travel.

All of this may seem astonishing, paranormal or even impossible to you. I am not asking you to believe me, but to carry out seriously your own work observing the connections between your dreams and reality. You will then see, when you have gathered enough oneiric and diurnal information, that future events are present in dreams well before they happen in reality. In fact, observing the connections between dreams and reality in this way shows that we are not living life in the sense that we believe. Everything seems to happen in reverse. That is to say that everything we experience in reality, we have already created on an energy/informational/vital level in dreams. It is as if in reality we only make events happen that we created alone or with other people in the energy world of dreams.

However, it seems equally clear that although dreams construct our reality, reality in turn influences dreams, since we are able to receive through our body, in a waking state, all kinds of influences which are mixed in with the energy fabric of dreams with which by ourselves we 'create' most of our life and future. This aspect of human life was very well known for example by the ancient Maya who taught the art of 'sowing and growing dreams'. It is also into this energy world of dreams that stands alongside our 'real world' that shamans of many traditions go into upon entering a trance. In this way they undergo changes at an energy level before the material manifestation of some events which they can also change the course of. I can also do the same thing directly while dreaming and in a dream state. That is to say that with their permission I enter into the dreams of the people that I train in order to help them sort out certain problems, if they are not experienced enough to do this themselves.

Despite all the tangible results obtained for millenniums by shamans of various traditions who use energy from dreams, there still exist in the West many researchers, notably in the field of oneiric lucidity, who think that dreams only exist in the head of the dreamer, who in this case dreams alone. Yet while it is true that some dreams only concern the dreamer and happen in his body and his head, an observation of the links between dreams and reality in a single dreamer quickly reveals that he does not dream alone and that in a dream state his body and mind exchange information and energy with the environment and other dreamers.

The marquis Hervey de Saint Denys, a western pioneer in the field of oneiric lucidity thought that everyone dreamt alone. However, Hervey de Saint Denys was a very gifted lucid dreamer and full of imagination when inventing experiments. In 1867 he wrote a work entitled: *Dreams and How to*

Guide Them[17] that describes his experiments in the field and which is still the bible for researchers of oneiric lucidity. His oeuvre is of great interest, even if despite the evidence of his own experiments he continued to think that he dreamt alone.

There exists as Robert Moss writes[18], a kind of psychic Internet. This is particularly active while dreaming. The existence of this 'psychic internet' allows our subconscious to exchange information, and for example to register environmental dangers, and to be up to date with the thoughts of individuals who might be a danger to us. It is thanks to this ability to exchange information when dreaming that I was able to be warned of the attacks in New York.

The dream that indicated the greatest danger that I have had during my life did indeed concern the attacks on the 11th September in New York. One night in July 2001 I woke up after having had a very clear dream in which I saw things like large

---

[17] Hervey de Saint Denys, *Des Rêves et des Moyens de les Diriger*, Editions Buenos Books International, www.buenosbooks.fr

[18] Robert Moss, *Dreaming True, How to dream your future and change your life for the better*, Pocket Books, New York, 2000

white shells falling on Manhattan buildings. I was watching this scene very calmly, and then I saw myself just as calmly walking with a crowd of Americans along a Manhattan street. The day before I had started to organise my September trip to New York and I had done some research on the Internet in order to find accommodation. This dream made me think a great deal. It was so strong, so special, but 'war in New York' seemed so unbelievable to me and completely improbable. Finally after hesitating for a long time, I decided to buy my plane ticket and to travel to New York in September 2001. I took this decision because, despite 'the war in New York' that this dream warned me of, I could also see that I was alive, that I had no problems, that I was walking among a crowd in a Manhattan street. Personally I apparently was not running any risk by travelling to New York, even in the case that the improbable 'war' indicated in the dream were to actually happen. On the 11th September 2001 I was therefore in Manhattan in accommodation that I had rented on 14th avenue to the East of the city. After working all morning I went out for lunch and I saw that there was no traffic in the neighbourhood. The road was filled with a crowd of pedestrians who were walking in silence in the direction of Brooklyn bridge. I joined them because I wanted to go in the same direction. While I was walking in this crowd I first thought that there was a festival that day. But quickly I sensed that it was not a festival atmosphere, but rather a terrible atmosphere of catastrophe. I then asked a police officer who was there why there was smoke in the distance around Battery Park. He said to me that there had been an attack and that the Twin Towers had been demolished. Suddenly the dream that I had had in July came to mind and I understood that, like in this dream, I was calmly walking among a crowd while 'a war was taking place in New York'. My dream of July, despite the fact that I had rationally considered it unlikely, had then turned out to be a real dream warning of catastrophe. This means that at the time I dreamt, these events were then already present at the energy state in the 'parallel world' of dreams, and maybe even well before the month of July. I myself picked up on them in July, as it is then that I started my preparations for travelling to New York in September. If I had not arranged to go to New York on that date, I probably would not have dreamed of these attacks. Indeed the very large majority of us dream of dangers that threaten us personally or that threaten loved ones and that matter to us in one way or another. Fortunately our brain filters subconscious information, otherwise with all the misery that still exists in our world, our nights would just be an infinite succession of terrible nightmares!

This example shows that through our dreams it is perfectly possible to be warned of all kinds of dangers and not only natural disasters. We can pick up during sleep (and in the case of very gifted people directly in a waking state) all kinds of information we need. In order for this to happen it is necessary to learn how to make better use of our ability to dream. This is easy using the method of observing the links between dreams and reality that I explain in this book.

By doing your own observational work, you will also be able to be warned in dreams of dangers that threaten you. You will even, as has happened to me, be able to be warned of the intentions of criminals, for example of burglars, and either frustrate them if that is possible, or limit the damage.

To give you every chance to develop your ability to sense the dangers of your environment it is also necessary, however, to respect some basic lifestyle rules. The first of these is to sleep enough. Indeed, when we do not sleep enough it is – nearly always – extremely difficult to remember dreams. It is also necessary to avoid as much as possible:

- stimulants such as coffee, alcohol, tea, meat, etc.

- drugs

- psychological medication: antidepressants, tranquillizers, etc. which often have the secondary effect of disturbing oneiric activity and often of purely and simply depriving ill people of the memory of their dreams.[19]

- too substantial dinners eaten shortly before sleeping.

- watching too much television, surfing the Internet too much, reading too much, or spending too long communicating by telephone or otherwise with too many people.

In these cases, your dreams will only be the 'digestion' of daily televisual, auditory and textual information, etc. (which is often completely useless), and you will have great difficulty accessing your own information. It will be 'drowned' in the flood of outside information which you have over loaded your head and body with. In such conditions, your dreams will not be real dreams from the deepest part within you, but just a mental bric-a-brac created by your conscious mind undergoing informational 'indigestion'. Unfortunately in modern times it is the lot of thousands of people to sleep each night after several hours spent absorbing television after a day without a moment's solitude. It is useful to know

---

[19] Accupuncture is very effective against depression and does not have the side effects of medication.

too that activities done just before going to sleep programme the brain to dream of certain subjects.

For that matter, at first during the experiment in order to gain better results, it would be ideal to sleep alone. Indeed, the bubbles of information-energy mix together, it is very difficult if you cannot sleep alone to tell the difference between what belongs to you and what doesn't. For example, a woman can regularly dream that she is bald and that she is very hairy if she sleeps with a partner with these characteristics. In the same way a man may dream, sometimes scaring him, that he has the feminine characteristics of his partner. Bodily sensations are often communicated between sleepers who share the same sleeping space!

Consequently it is a lot easier to get to know well your own oneiric ground, by sleeping alone at the start of the experiment. Afterwards, it will be easier to know what does and does not belong to you on an informational and vibratory level. If you are normally single, you will be able to observe how during sexual relations with a new person, the content of your dreams changes a lot and that unusual information from your partner enters your informational system. You will also pick up variations in the level of your energy and many more things. For example, a depressed, sad or anxious state immediately after even successful sex, or the day after, most often indicates that the energy exchange with your partner has been unfavourable to you.

An interesting experiment to do, but not advised for depressed people, consists in isolating yourself for several days while fasting or eating lightly and having baths. After this period of isolation, you will be able to sense the difference a lot better between our own energy and that of people, animals and places with which we will be in contact again.

If you wish to use your dreams in order to be warned of dangers there is one last thing to point out: do not read horror or violent books: do not watch violent and disaster films: avoid televisual information of this kind above all at night before going to sleep. All of this influences your brain, causes dreams with false warnings of disasters and greatly contributes to depriving you of your natural ability to 'dream truthfully'.

Lastly I would like to underline how important it is to be calm. The calmer we are the greater chance we have of having real dreams that come from our deepest selves, and of communicating better with our body and our subconscious. Therefore do everything you can to avoid stress or to relax if you haven't been able to avoid it. Also at night make a habit of having a relaxing herbal tea (of good quality and without pesticides); for example lavender, chamomile, lime, etc. You can also diffuse in your room calming essential oils which you like the smell of.

By following all this advice you will learn in a natural way and safely, the language of your dreams. You will learn how better to communicate with your body, and you will also learn how to distinguish which among your warning dreams are real warning dreams, that relate to reality, and those that are simply nightmares, caused by reasons that you will have learnt to detect, and which I am now going to talk to you about, in order to save you a lot of time in your personal work.

CHAPTER 6:

WHAT TRIGGERS FALSE ONEIRIC WARNINGS OF NATURAL DISASTERS?

We have spoken above about the attempts that were made in England, America and in Belgium to use the populations' dreams in order to warn inhabitants of environmental risks and thereby save lives. We have seen that the natural disaster dream recording bureaux were very quickly submerged by a great number of dreams which nearly all (fortunately) turned out to be false warnings, simply nightmares. Instead of continuing to try to understand why so many dreams were only false warnings, and finding another more efficient way of proceeding, sadly these trials were ended. To my knowledge no one sought to understand why the population as a whole is so susceptible to nightmares and how this situation could be improved.

I think that it was an excellent idea to create bureaux for oneiric observation of disasters, but the way in which this observation was set up doomed the experiment to failure. Indeed, to my knowledge, only the dreams were recorded, independently of the dreamers, their lifestyle, the places where they had dreamed, and the many reasons causing the false warnings of disasters.

Firstly it would have been possible to proceed by recording lots of dreams, in order to find the people most able truly to sense current natural disasters, and also the people least prone to nightmares. Secondly the recording bureaux could have decided to work mainly with the most able people. These people are increasingly rare nowadays, whereas people prone to dreams with false warnings of disaster have become more and more numerous. It is not difficult to understand why. In the passages that follow through my research I am going to explain to you how I have been able to understand what causes most of these dreams giving false warnings of disasters.

By reading the explanations I am now going to give you about nightmares (or dreams of false warnings), you will be able to understand what the conditions are that so often cause disaster dreams in so many people, dreams that fortunately for us will only happen in their own psyche.

The explanations that I am now going to give you are a result of my long experience. But quite clearly in this field there is still a lot to discover. It is also true that despite extremely bad oneiric conditions, in rare cases some dreamers may still have real dreams that may save their lives by warning them of dangers that threaten them. It is often the case that such dreamers believe that they have benefited from a 'divine' intervention, for example that of a guardian angel or a dead relative.

For ease of exposition I have classed false warning nightmares into several groups. This list of nightmares is not exhaustive. For example I have left out 'shamanic' nightmares which are linked to oneiric contact with 'parallel' worlds and which these days in the West are beyond the understanding and the experience of 'normal' man. Modern Western man has cut himself off from nature and his subconscious to such an extent that I may even have taken a risk in mentioning this kind of dream here! But that is the end of this digression. I will now talk about bodily nightmares, nightmares of the mind, and nightmares linked to energy.

1) Disaster false warning nightmares triggered by the body

These nightmares are becoming increasingly prevalent nowadays and the main reason for them is disturbances of the digestive system. In ancient civilisations techniques were practised in order to keep the digestive system in good health. It was indeed normal to fast regularly and to cleanse the intestines using water. Thanks to these preventative measures people were able to keep their digestive system in good health, clean their intestines and their body, and regularly free themselves of toxins.

These days very few people fast, and even fewer people have good intestinal hygiene. In the case of intestinal blockage nearly everyone is now happy to swallow some laxatives without ever bothering to cleanse themselves correctly. This combined with the stress of modern life, inactivity and a denatured diet, means that from a certain age (and sometimes very early for some people), the intestines can no longer work correctly as they have a hardened layer of non-evacuated matter. The intestinal flora is therefore unbalanced, causing fermentation, gas, aerophagia and many other unpleasant effects throughout the body. If you wish to know more about intestinal hygiene, I invite you to read *Témoignage sur les bienfaits de l'hygiène intestinale* (A report on the benefits of intestinal hygiene)[20] written by Laure Goldbright, in which she explains how to practise intestinal hygiene and the many benefits that it can bring.

If you wish to dream better, the cleanliness and the functioning of your digestive organs is of prime importance. A disturbed digestive system causes very vivid nightmares because the body expresses extreme malaise in this way, due to blood intoxication, poorer circulation and poor oxygenation of the blood, which is itself caused by

---

20 *Témoignage sur les Bienfaits de l'hygiène intestinale*, Laure Goldbright, Buenos Books International, Paris. Also available as an electronic version and in Spanish and Italian.

breathing being hampered by the pressure exerted by the stomach and intestines, which are swollen with gas. Sometimes even, a digestive nightmare is triggered by occasional indigestion or food intolerance. Keeping a notebook of dreams and reality where we note down what we have eaten can help us to understand which foods do not suit our bodies. Foods that the body cannot tolerate often cause nightmares that betray a serious and very real malaise.

Man has lost contact with nature and his own body to such an extent that very often he does not sense in a waking state that his body is disturbed, that a food, drink or a place does not suit his body. Fortunately in many cases there are still nightmares to sound the alarm before it is too late, but it is still necessary to be aware of them without being scared.

In most people whose digestive system is very clogged up and disturbed I have noticed that they either completely forget their dreams or they have many dreams and recurrent nightmares of natural disasters. These nightmares may happen every night, generally at the same time. They are often accompanied by shivers, little hot flushes, sweating and difficulty getting to sleep. They can also on the contrary be accompanied by excessive sleepiness with unbridled oneiric activity. Some people have recurrent dreams of human slaughter, that is to say dreams in which there is a lot of blood due to all kinds of disastrous events, different each night. According to Chinese medicine this kind of dream is due to a malfunction in spleen energy.

Other people may have recurrent dreams of disasters in which they lose their legs or they see many people with severed legs, very often at the knee. Following my observations it seems to me that this is due to the fact that circulation in the legs is hampered 'mechanically' by the stomach which is full of gas. (In reality: these people have feet that are nearly always cold).

Some people dream regularly of disasters in which they lose their sight, arms, etc. Blockage of the digestive system is a real disaster for the body, because not only does it cause restriction of blood and nerve circulation, but also progressive intoxication of the body which can no longer breathe properly, feed itself properly and cleanse itself effectively of waste and toxins. I have observed that people suffering from acidity in their digestive system are prone to terrible nightmares of nuclear disasters or wars in which the weapons used are caustic chemical weapons.

Despite all these real bodily disturbances there are people who are so insensitive to themselves that they put up with this state while believing they are in good health and thinking it is normal that their gut and stomach is always swollen. Owing to the state of their stomach, it is as if they are anaesthetized. They live well above their vital capacity and in some cases they no longer remember their dreams or nightmares. Clearly in this case it is far better to have nightmares and feel bad in one's body. At least it would be advisable to do something in order to remedy all these problems and regain good health and vitality instead of living 'at a minimum vital level'. Eliminating this kind of dream, as you know, is very easy. All it takes (as Laure Goldbright explains in her book mentioned above), is to fast, have colonic irrigations and have a good lifestyle. Sadly natural and allopathic laxatives do not clean the intestines, they only make the situation worse.

Currently digestive problems are the main causes of nightmares with false warnings of disasters. They affect most of the western adult population who eat increasingly denatured food and in an increasingly stressful atmosphere. It should also be taken into account that everything we eat is also full of information. I will allow you to guess the effect that the consumption of meat from animals that have been mistreated and sometimes killed in horrible conditions has on our informational system.

After this major cause of corporeal nightmares comes another quite common and even more unknown cause which is a badly positioned atlas (the first cervical vertebra). According to research carried out by René Schümperli very many people have a badly positioned atlas and in those who have suffered trauma it is very badly positioned. René Schümperli also observed that mothers with a displaced atlas give birth to children with badly positioned atlases. It is easy to understand by opening an anatomy book that a badly positioned atlas hugely disturbs blood flow in the brain as well as nerve impulses. This is liable to cause recurring disaster dreams. This problem is, however, very easy to fix now thanks to René Schümperli's invention which allows the atlas to be put back into its proper position without risk or pain. You can find more information on the inventor's website and by reading the books that he has published.[21]

As well as these two main causes the other malaises of the body often all cause dreams of natural disasters, wars, fire, etc. The body uses nature's language in order to make itself understood. Moreover as the body is itself part of nature it only understands and speaks this language.

On this subject I would like to share a dream I had one night and which really affected me. In this dream I found myself faced with a magnificent tiger and I asked this question: "But what is a

---

[21] http://www.atlasprofilax.ch

tiger?" In the dream I received this quite unexpected reply: "A tiger is a cosmos, and each cell in his body is a star". I conclude from this that every living organism is a cosmos like the tiger in my dream. When we try to observe the connections between our dreams and our reality we come to realise that our body is also a cosmos; it is a whole interior world with its landscapes, rivers, mountains, inhabitants, bad weather and natural disasters, that is visible in a dream state. Disturbances in our body often trigger nightmares that show us 'full scale' natural disasters.

Such dreams, impressive and full of imagery as they are, do not foretell disasters in our outside environment. However, in reality, 'disasters' (disorders) have indeed taken place inside our own bodily universe.

For example at one point in my life I started to dream that I was in the streets of a town, struggling to climb mountains of sand several metres high that had overrun the area. This dream repeated itself every night. Did it predict a sand storm in Paris? No! Seeing this town that was more than real, with its streets, cars and inhabitants, my body was telling me that I had to stop the silicium supplement that I had been taking for some time and that did not agree with me. It was therefore not a recurrent dream foretelling a natural disaster, but a recurrent dream indicating, in the form of mountains of sand clogging up the 'arteries' of a town, that I had a disorder in my body. Indeed sand contains silicium and all I had to do was stop taking this supplement in order for this dream that had become recurrent to disappear, enabling me to avoid certain health problems.

In the same order of phenomena, fever, for example, can trigger nightmares which feature terrible droughts causing depopulation and the death of thousands of people (who in fact often represent cells). Inflammations can trigger nightmares of terrible fires. Kidney problems can cause dreams of disastrous and uncontrollable floods. [22] Problems related to blood, its composition and its circulation can trigger dreams featuring water courses, such as rivers in which people who are swimming are too fat (often an indication of cholesterol) or in which boats have navigational problems. The water in these rivers may be dirty, which is an indication of poisoning. In our body, that sometimes fights against invading microbes, there are also terrible wars that we can see in dreams, often without great emotion.

When we find ourselves in a given environment our mind watches with the eyes, smells with the nose, hears with the ears, but the body detects all kinds of other information through its whole

---

[22] Or also uncontrollable overflowing basins, baths, household washing machines, taps etc.

surface. The way in which the body senses the outside environment and all that we do to it 'blindly' can also trigger natural disaster nightmares. For example, thanks to his notebook one of my students was able to observe that his electroacupuncture sessions were triggering earthquake dreams. Electroacupuncture also triggers this kind of dream in me. As I have never in reality experienced an earthquake and what can be felt in the legs in that moment, I make the assumption that my body has received through its inherited emotions the memory of the experience of my ancestors (recent and distant) who nearly all lived in the south of Italy, a region which is subject to this kind of natural disaster. It seems that we arrive in the world with a memory already installed in our body (or in our mind?), that allows us to benefit from some of our ancestor's experiences, but also, sadly, to continue to suffer traumatic information and emotions lived by them.

Modern psychoanalysis has looked into this question and has proved that there exists transgenerational transmission of certain traumas.

Anne Ancelin Schützenberger, a psychotherapist and group analyst, has been able to confirm, through her professional work, the existence of a kind of psychological inheritance that Freud, whom she quotes, [23] called 'archaic inheritance ':

"The archaic heritage of mankind includes not only dispositions, but also ideational contents, memory-traces of the experiences of former generations."[24]

In a very interesting work called Aïe mes aïeux! Anne Ancelin Schützenberger gives many examples from her research which show the existence of transgenerational psychological links. As far as nightmares are concerned, many examples are given that concern people's descendants who have experienced traumatic events, whether or not the people having these nightmares were consciously aware of the events. She writes:

"The existence of transgenerational transmission of serious traumas which are not spoken about -or which have been forgotten- such as war traumas (gas, drownings or near-drownings, tortures, rape of a parent, brother or war comrade) has been proven.

---

[23] Ancelin Schützenberger Anne, *Aïe mes aïeux!*, Paris, Desclée de Brouwer, 1999, p. 15.

[24] FREUD Sigmund, *Moses and montheism*, 1939, Hogarth Press, 1939, p. 163.

Nothing we know from a psychological, physiological or neurological point of view explains how something can worry generations of the same family."[25]

The solution that she proposes in the case of such nightmares is psychotherapy that consists in researching what happened in the family history, in order to make people aware of the problem so that it can be treated correctly, by forgiveness or by forgetting, in order to avoid trouble for future generations.[26] But it is also possible to resolve this problem otherwise by acting on dreams.

One of my students had regular dreams of tidal waves in which she would die, having drowned. This caused her a lot of anguish as she lived near the sea. Her notebook of dreams revealed that these dreams happened above all after colonic irrigation. Her body interpreted the feeling of the stomach being full of water as drowning. We have done some research and learnt that one of her ancestors died at sea. In this case the information

---

[25] Ancelin Schützenberger Anne, *op. cit.*, p. 64.

[26] Aïe, mes aïeux*!: Liens transgénérationnels, secrets de famille, syndrome d'anniversaire, transmission des traumatismes et pratique du génosociogramme*, Desclée de Brouwer, 1998, Anne Ancelin Schützenberger

seems to have been transferred to the following generations. This person therefore possessed somewhere (in her gene pool? in her psychological inheritance?) the memory of the bodily sensation caused by drowning. This memory manifested itself in a dream following the bodily sensation of 'too much water'.

As you can see in these few examples, knowing what has happened in reality to a person and sometimes even what has happened to their ancestors and close relatives is key to understanding whether nightmares are premonitory or not.

One day in my doctor's waiting room a patient told me his recurrent dreams of car accidents, in which he just managed to escape from the car. Intuitively I sensed that he was repeating a family trauma and I asked him if anyone in his family had died in these circumstances. It so happened that many of his close relatives had died in car accidents. I encouraged him to do personal work in order to free himself from these unpleasant nightmares and also in order to neutralise the danger in a dream state.

As we will now see there also exist nightmares triggered by psychological suffering which are not caused by traumas or psychic inheritances, but reflect the dreamers' interior conflicts.

2) Natural disaster nightmares caused by the mind

Here we are entering the special area of disaster dreams (natural or not) including accidents involving transport (cars, buses, planes, trains, motorbikes, boats, bikes and even monocycles!), accidents related to water (tidal waves, leaks and all kinds of overflowing, flooding rivers, etc.) wind destruction, wars, disasters linked to the earth (earthquakes, volcanic eruptions, landslides). All such dreams first bring to mind damage that has happened to the dreamer's home or just to parts of the home. I have called this section 'nightmares of the mind', but I could also have called it 'psychological nightmares' or 'nightmares of the psyche'. It doesn't matter!

It is worth remembering that psychological malaise tends to trigger very striking and extremely disturbing natural disaster nightmares.

We can stop them happening by discovering or rediscovering, alone or with outside help, a psychological balance that has been lost for various reasons. Keeping a dream and reality notebook can also help you. But it is also sometimes necessary to make some changes in our lives, for which courage is often needed: for example, leaving the financial security of a job that doesn't suit us for another that would suit us a lot better, or even ending a relationship that doesn't suit us, or even leaving a place or country in which you do not feel well.

Keeping a dream and reality notebook allows you to get to know well your own psychological terrain, and helps you take steps in real life in order to accelerate the recovery of the psyche. This can be done together with another therapy which would be all the more effective.

When you understand your ‘psychological terrain’ and the kind of recurrent nightmares that it causes, you will be able to recognise these disaster nightmares that are merely a representation of an ‘interior psychological nightmare’ and distinguish them from real warning dreams. Warning dreams are often marked by great emotional calm, while psychological nightmares are often marked by intense emotions and conflicts. Here are several examples of disaster dreams that are related to psychological problems:

Accident and disfigurement:

A person dreamt regularly of car accidents in which she was completely disfigured. Thanks to her dream and reality notebook we were able to understand that this person was in reality suffering from not being in her proper place in society, that she was playing a 'role' that her family environment demanded by working professionally in a job that didn't suit her at all. She was definitely no longer herself. Her family environment had psychologically 'disfigured' her. Admitting this psychological suffering allowed her to live a life more in line with her real needs; her nightmares disappeared and her health improved.

Tidal wave and drowning:

Another person dreamt that she had been swept away by a gigantic tidal wave before the start of a period in her life of intense questioning, doubt and unease.

Aeroplane accident:

A highly qualified person who was passionate about her job, but who had been unemployed for years as she couldn't find a job matching her abilities, ended up accepting a job far below her abilities and which didn't relate to her studies and her social environment. Shortly before accepting this job she had very frightening nightmares in which she saw herself flying a plane alone that suddenly crashed to the ground, killing her. In this case it wasn't a premonitory dream, rather a dream indicating that her psyche was suffering. This person had in a way, 'fallen from a great height' in terms of her professional aspirations, and her dreams revealed symbolically the intensity of her psychological suffering.

A sudden shake up of a person's certainties, ways of thinking and habits can trigger dreams of earthquakes, or such dreams may be the warning of this kind of malaise.

I am not going to dwell on this kind of nightmare because it is very easy to find examples of them everywhere in psychology books. These are the kind of nightmares that have (and have always been) the most studied by psychotherapists. Also there is currently a tendency too often to attribute nightmares to psychological causes, although psychological nightmares are not, for most of us, the most common nightmares.

A third cause for nightmares often being wrongly attributed to psychological problems is the energy environment of the sleeper.

3) Nightmares giving false warnings of natural disasters relating to energy disturbances in the sleeper's environment:

As well as having a physical dimension our body also has an energy dimension. Energy currents go through our body, which is in a permanent energy exchange with its natural environment and with the living beings that surround it: human beings, animals and even plants. The earth also has an energy dimension. Just as energy meridian lines cover our body, the earth has an energy network that is called the

Hartmann network by geobiologists. Some places where the telluric energy lines meet can be very beneficial for people who stay there and they can recharge their body with energy, while in other places people may simply die if they expose themselves to them every day or night for years.

Almost all of us have lost all conscious sensitivity to these energy disturbances and there are many people who think that such a concept is ridiculous. However, even if we don't believe in it, our body continues to sense these energies and in most cases it is our dreams, but in the most serious cases nightmares, that warn us that something is not right energetically. By observing the connections between dreams and reality, we quickly see that one of the main objectives of dreams is the preservation of energy, meaning vitality, growth, i.e. life. Some domestic animals have kept intact this sensitivity to the energy of places. Cats for example are known to love sitting down on energy points that are harmful for man, but not for them. They even have the ability to transform these harmful energies.

How these telluric and cosmic energy networks worked seems to have been understood a lot better in ancient civilisations than in modern times. Temples, dwellings and other buildings were built taking into account the ground's energy data. Places of worship were chosen above all because they were energetically 'special' from a telluric and cosmic point of view. Because of this energetic specificity, religious beliefs, gods and rites changed often throughout history while the places of worship stayed the same.

In modern times this would not be considered by most contemporary Western architects who are often ignorant of the earth's dense energy network and its effects on living beings, and who do not think of testing the telluric as well as cosmic energy reality of places before constructing buildings. Besides, even if they wanted to, it seems that the knowledge required to select places of worship and construct temples has been lost.

The temples of ancient Greece, Rome and Egypt were built in high energy places, like other ancient spiritual sites throughout the world. It is no accident that even today their remains are like 'magnets' that attract crowds who continue to recharge there without knowing it. Whether the people who form these crowds believe in God or not or in the existence of telluric energy, their bodies benefit from these places. If their energy properties are still intact these are very attractive places where we feel very good, joyful and at peace, because we can recharge there. All these positive emotions are indeed mainly caused by the abundance of energy that the body feels in places where it can recharge with excellent quality energy.

In the West, in 'New Age' circles, the Chinese art of Feng Shui is now in fashion. This art helps to manage and channel the energy of buildings for the health and prosperity of the people who live and work in them. In France geobiologists offer the same kind of services which are called in this case not Feng Shui but 'energy harmonisation' or energy 'rebalancing'.

Although these practices, still known these days, can make a real improvement in the lives of the people that benefit from them, they seem to me to be only 'scraps' of far deeper knowledge which were used for example in ancient China or by the priests of ancient Egypt.

Even if it is no longer possible to act with the efficiency of the ancient Egyptians in constructing buildings of high energy power or in accumulating energy in certain places and in certain objects, to my knowledge it is still possible for anyone who tries to develop their own natural ability, to sense the energy quality of places in which we stand. No war, cataclysm or withheld information can take this away from us, because it is a natural ability that we all have and which is easy to develop by applying the very simple method explained in this book.

Apparently it seems that in ancient Rome this human ability had already been dulled, as we know that the ancient Romans used the sensitivity of animals in order to test the energy quality of places where they wished to build. We know for example that the ancient Romans allowed geese to live for a year on land on which they wanted to construct a building.

Then these geese were killed and depending on the state of their intestines the ancient Romans decided whether or not to construct on the land where the geese had lived.

We are all, without exception, affected by the energy quality of the places in which we live, whatever our conscious sensibility to the energy quality of our environment. In other words, even if we don't believe in it and even if we don't consciously perceive anything of the energy aspect of existence, that does not stop our body from being disturbed or even stimulated in its energetic functioning depending on the places where we are staying. People may fall ill and sometimes die because of repeated exposure to energy that is harmful to life: for example in their bedroom, or in their place of work. In Paris the energy atmosphere of some department stores is very harmful to the physical and psychological health of the shop assistants. It also leads clients who are sensitive enough not to linger there, or those like me, not to go there at all if it is possible to buy what is sold there on the Internet. They are particularly exhausting and harmful places and despite this, there are plenty of people who love to spend their time there and feel no discomfort at all!

From my research, I have been able to observe that many natural disaster dreams (which never happen in reality) are quite simply caused by energetic disturbances in the dreamer's bedroom. Therefore if you are prone to recurrent nightmares, it is necessary above all to check if they are triggered by energy disturbances in your room. In order to do this either enlist the services of a specialist who will come with detection instruments, or ask someone in your family circle to help you, a person who (like me and many others) is able in a waking state to sense all this naturally with their body. You can also achieve this by yourself, using trial and error, by changing the position of your bed, or by going to sleep in another room and comparing the quality of your sleep each time you change, until you regain a refreshing sleep that is free of nightmares.

I have been able to observe that if there is an energy disturbance in the place where a person sleeps, he may go to bed very tired, ready to sleep, but he may not manage to sleep despite his fatigue. It seems to me that this is due to the fact that his body, which is disturbed by the poor energy quality of his environment, remains tense and does not manage to achieve the level of muscular relaxation necessary for sleep. In such cases all it takes for people who believe they have become ‘insomniac’, following a move for example, is simply to change the position of the bed in order to sleep normally and regain a peaceful and refreshing sleep.

It is often the case that when going on holiday to the mountains in order to relax, some people come back more tired because they haven't been able to sleep properly there. Often that is quite simply due to the fact that their bed was badly positioned in relation to the water courses near where they were trying to sleep. In order to sleep well in the mountains the bed must be placed in the direction of the natural flow of torrents. If this precaution is taken, sleeping near a rushing stream or a river is pleasant, refreshing and beneficial, instead of the cause of insomnia. All it takes for these people who have suffered insomnia during their holiday in the mountains is to return home to regain normal sleep.

Conversely, for other people, insomnia, or sleep that is hardly refreshing at all and filled with recurring nightmares, systematically ends when they are away. In such cases there is a strong possibility that the cause of the nightmares and insomnia may be found in the normal bedroom of the sleeper. It is then sometimes necessary to change the position of the bed and furniture, take the mirrors down (or cover them before going to sleep if you can't take them down), avoid having metal and electrical objects near the bed (or even in bed), in order for people to regain a peaceful sleep and better health when sleeping in their own homes.

I have observed that when the body is energetically disturbed during sleep, this often triggers recurrent nightmares that last several months, even years. Then these nightmares often end, although sleep becomes less and less refreshing and it takes longer and longer and is more difficult to get to sleep, sometimes leading to the taking of sleeping pills or tranquilisers. After some time, which varies from one person to the next, illness can take its hold. It becomes as chronic as it is unexplainable from a medical point of view, and sometimes leads to death. There exist, for example, buildings that are energetically 'unhealthy', in which most of the inhabitants die inexplicably of the same pathologies that also affect their pets. Michel Moine and Jean-Louis Degaudenzi give a striking example of this in the geobiological manual. There was a building in Paris, on rue Blanche, where all the inhabitants were affected by harmful waves, some even dying, before the cause was discovered and resolved.[27]

---

[27] *Manual de Energias Teluricas, Experimentos Energéticos Para Vivir Mejor*, Michel Moine y Jean-Louis Degaudenzi, p. 51. Title of the French edition: *Guide de Géobiologie*, Christian de Bartillat, 1993

Electrical appliances such as alarm clocks, mobile telephones, televisions, computers and sockets that are near the body also disturb our energy even though very few people are still capable of feeling discomfort or malaise upon waking.

Although energy disturbances which discomfort the body are not sensed consciously upon waking, there are still many people who are warned by the body that it is suffering these energy disturbances. Natural disaster dreams or dreams featuring attacks are triggered, in order to make the conscious mind aware of the need to do something in order to preserve the integrity of the body's energy.

Having electrical devices near the bed should absolutely be avoided. If this cannot be avoided disconnect televisions and computers before going to sleep and cover their screens with a bit of tissue, because surfaces which reflect light in the direction of the sleeper disturb sleep and dreams.

Personally I am too sensitive to my energy environment to be able to sleep with any electrical device on my bedside table or near my bed! Likewise, through experience you will come to realise that having metal objects in your bed should be avoided (for example spring mattresses!); also the presence of mirrors in your bedroom and even more things that you will be able to detect by testing the quality of your sleep through your observational work of your dreams and reality.

Somebody who was complaining of recurrent dreams in which she was attacked by bats that bit her all over her body made these nightmares simply go away, by following my advice to remove a broken electrical device that was on the bedside table, near her head and which was seriously disturbing her energy, without her being aware of it in a waking state.

As we have seen, provided we have managed to find the concrete cause, this kind of nightmare is one of the easiest to eliminate. It is necessary either to sleep elsewhere, change the position of the bed or enlist the services of competent specialists in order to improve the energy quality of places. The disasters shown by this kind of nightmare aren't events that will actually occur in the real world, but rather warnings of disasters concerning the health of the sleeper, that will certainly occur if they do not take the necessary steps to resolve these energy disturbances that affect their body during sleep.

By keeping a dream and reality notebook in the manner that I explain in this book, you will be able to detect dangers to your health which are a result of your energy environment, before it is too late. Babies, who are far more sensitive to their energy environment than most adults, may cry a lot and be constantly ill because of the place where we make them sleep. Often all it takes is to change the position of their cradle for them to feel better and stop crying during the night. Also, young children sometimes feel anxious in their bedrooms because of energetic disturbances and regularly seek refuge in their parents' room. Sometimes it is just the harmful energy of certain places that makes their inhabitants anxious and nervous and that leads them to take lots of medicines, whereas all they need to do is become aware of the harmfulness of the energy of the place where they live and to resolve this.

Doing the work on dreams that I suggest can also develop sensitivity to the energy of places directly in a waking state, because the body and diurnal consciousness have re-established communication. It is very useful to sense with your body the places that do not suit you; you can then leave them instead of becoming pointlessly exhausted. There are places that are aesthetically magnificent and energetically disastrous. For me personally, the energetic quality of places is more important when choosing, than the physical appearance of places. The ideal would be to live in an environment that is physically beautiful and comfortable, healthy and energetically invigorating.

Sleeping in some places can trigger nightmares due to the emotions of the people or animals that lived there in the past. Such nightmares are the recovery of information from the past; they relate neither to the dreamer nor to an event that will happen in reality. These disaster dreams are simply created by the brain using energetic/emotional/informational type information that is picked up by the whole body. It is no accident that in ancient civilisations there were many rituals for the purification of places. People were aware of this aspect of life. Sleeping in buildings built on ancient abattoirs, in houses where crimes or other acts of violence were committed and on old battle grounds, etc., would for example be avoided. And if this could not be avoided the services of a competent specialist would be enlisted in order to try to purify these places.

To conclude the section on nightmares with false warnings of disasters, I am going to speak about post-traumatic nightmares and transgenerational traumatic nightmares.

4) Post-traumatic nightmares and transgenerational traumatic nightmares:

People who have been traumatised by real natural disasters may for some time afterwards, in dreams, repeat the scenes that traumatised them.

Then this fades away, but then reappears if an event in reality or simply stress reactivates this 'painful' memory. In this case the disaster dreams would clearly almost always be false warnings.

This kind of recurrent nightmare is sadly far more difficult to eliminate than other kinds of false warning nightmares and they can even be transferred from generation to generation. In this way distant descendants may in dreams repeat traumatic scenes from wars, natural disasters or accidents that they haven't directly experienced, but whose memory has been passed down to them by their close or distant ancestors. In the case of recurrent disaster nightmares, if they are triggered neither by health problems, nor energy disturbances in the sleeper's environment, nor by a psychological malaise, it is then necessary to look into their ancestors. If the person who has these nightmares regularly sleeps with someone else, the ancestors of the person who shares the same bed should be looked into.

Indeed, through observation of my dreams and reality, and also by observing many people, I have come to understand that in a couple there is an intense informational exchange due to the proximity of the bodies in a same bed during the night, and also due to sexual relations which mix energies. Sometimes it is the most sensitive person in the couple (most often the woman) who has the transgenerational nightmares, in place of his/her partner. The same happens in a family, owing to communal living and blood-ties there is an intense exchange of information between all the members of the family. Hence the interest in listening to the dreams of all the members of the family, and also in observing our pets, who although they don't speak our language, can also in their way communicate information that could save our lives.

When the transgenerational cause of nightmares is determined we can act directly in dreams in order to resolve this kind of trauma at source. Some psychologists are also interested in this matter, and many people worldwide have looked into the subject of transgenerational transmission of psychological traumas. It is easy to find them on the Internet, but it is perfectly possible to manage by yourself by doing personal work on dreams. For that matter, other techniques such as hypnosis or shamanism can sometimes be very effective in freeing oneself from a transgenerational trauma. If you decide to use your own initiative you will see that simply taking an interest in your dreams, observing the links with your reality and allowing the emotions of dreams to reach your diurnal consciousness will help you to understand better who you are and to heal your psyche by rediscovering the true path that you should have followed in your life, and your real personality.

We have now come to the end of the section on false warning dreams and their causes. Stress in all its forms is another element that is a factor in all kinds of nightmares (those that I have mentioned and all the others), stress makes them worse and triggers them.

For example a very anxious friend told me that some time ago his wife had started dreaming every night that her two children were dying. They would be knocked down by a car, kidnapped and killed, crushed in a lift accident, struck by a deadly illness, etc. In brief his wife saw her two children die every night and these frightening dreams woke her up filling her with fear. In fact it turned out that these were only stress dreams. The dreamer was changing her job and she was going to have to take on new responsibilities that were causing her a lot of stress. As this mother was also quite naturally worried about her young children, her stress transformed in her dreams into attacks or accidents concerning her children. They were therefore false warning dreams of dangers triggered by an extremely stressful situation in reality. In dreams stress often bears upon what we hold closest emotionally or on our everyday flaws and fears. For example an unscrupulous thief might dream that the police arrest him when he goes to sleep in a state of stress; a miser might dream that his money is being stolen, etc.

Therefore, avoid stress at all costs. Avoid stimulants and learn to relax. We can thereby avoid triggering nightmares, those that I have discussed above and all the other kinds of nightmares, which might not feature disasters but disturb sleep.

You will have understood, on reading this chapter concerning false warning dreams, why the idea of creating disaster dream recording bureaux was destined to fail. Too many people eat badly, live with stress and worries, and sleep in modern housing which has been constructed despite knowledge concerning energy fields, not ignoring the fact that the media constantly bombard us with images of violence, horror, bloodshed and disasters. If it is the case that it is with the energy from dreams (meaning life) that we first of all construct our reality then reality also influences dreams. Consequently someone who watches a horror film for example before going to sleep, 'programmes' his brain to dream of horror. In other words they put themselves in the energetic environment and the psychological conditions to dream of horrors, at least during the first hours of the night.

Consequently if you spend your time watching, hearing and reading all kinds of horrors, you can expect to have dreams and nightmares influenced by your daily activities! On the other hand you therefore know what should be done to have pleasant dreams, and also to benefit from your sleeping time instead of wasting it with sordid dreams conditioned by the media!

A brain that is constantly bombarded with disastrous information, will in all likelihood create disaster dreams. Indeed, there are so many ready-made disasters in memories! Furthermore, people who overload their brains with audiovisual information and do not allow themselves periods of silence (that often make them afraid), have 'dreams' that aren't really dreams, but rather residues of the "digestion" of information from the day before, that has saturated their brain. In this case there is permanent information indigestion, which deprives the person of his real ability to dream and of the possibility of entering into contact with his body and also his subconscious.

These days many people suffer, without being aware of it from real information indigestion, consisting of images and messages of disasters, wars, violence and horrors.

Personally, a very long time ago I took the necessary steps in order to preserve my true ability to dream: I no longer have a television and I protect my psyche as much as possible from 'the news' and films, books and shows that are psychologically unhealthy and which reduce vitality and the chances of having pleasant restorative or creative dreams. These things also reduce the likelihood of being warned of real dangers that threaten us in our environment! When I go to the cinema it is almost always in my dreams. The landscapes are grandiose, as are the light, colours and the music and I wake up in a good mood, full of energy, information and projects.

CONCLUSION

Through the channel of our body the psyche can access all the information from its environment in real time. Our conscious mind acts mainly as a filter which is configured according to our conscious interests of the time. If our brain didn't filter the multitude of information which our body and subconscious constantly receives, we might go mad and dream constantly of all the disasters that are happening in the world and which do not threaten us directly.

At present, modern man's ‘filter’ has really closed itself off from its natural environment, only allowing a very small amount of information concerning the energy of places. However given that we are nearly all very interested in staying alive, our ‘filter’ can therefore easily be ‘reprogrammed’ to allow the transfer of important oneiric information for our survival. For this, it is necessary to do the observational work on dreams and reality that is proposed in this book.

Natural disasters are, without exception, dreamt of when they concern us personally or when they concern people who are emotionally close to us. All over the world people must make the effort to explore their oneiric world in order to communicate better with their subconscious and their body, which are always there, like guardian angels, to help them to survive effectively. As far as animals are concerned, it would be very helpful for us to observe them more, but in the field of disaster forecasting they will never be able to equal the brain of a human being which has been trained to use its oneiric abilities. Indeed, animals don't seem to have the ability to sense dangers that don't have a natural cause, but are the result of human activities. For example, in towns and cities, a cat's instinct doesn't work to survive car traffic. Likewise, animals do not run away before a nuclear disaster, whereas a trained dreamer may be warned of this kind of disaster. It seems to me that animals are not able to detect through their subconscious, whether a plane or any means of transport has a technical problem. On the other hand I know that a dreamer who has been trained in the method that I have explained in this book, will be able to sense before getting on a plane if it is going to arrive safe and sound at its destination, or for example, if the plane has technical problems.

Succeeding in doing this is very simple. All it takes is to keep a dream and reality notebook as indicated in this book. Through this exercise you can learn to be familiar with your oneiric universe and see how our vital force constantly pushes us into the near or distant future. Therefore it is very simple to know whether you are going to arrive at your destination safely by plane or boat. Pay attention to your dreams before leaving (one or two weeks before) and whether in your dreams your life continues normally. For example, if you start to dream of the place you are travelling to, the things you will do there, the clothes you will wear and the people you will meet there, your journey will go well.

I am very happy to have shared the fruit of my research in this field with you and I hope that this book has interested you.

For those that want to go further I regularly organise courses that are announced on my site and I also give lectures on other aspects of dreams and for example on dreams and innovation.

www.amancini.com

I also train several people a year individually, for a period from 6 months to a year, to help them develop faster and more easily. I also help people with all kinds of problems. For example, I can also find lost objects thanks to my dreams. I can be contacted by email at the following address:

info@amancini.com

P.S.: When I finished this book I met a researcher who assured me that according to his astronomical calculations, on the 6th June 2012 there would be a calamity due to the transit of

Venus, and that a third of the world's population would die due to this transit. I did some research on the Internet and I noticed that there is information on this subject, but also announcements of other calamities on other dates, notably in December 2012.

Personally up to now I haven't dreamt of such an event, neither in Paris nor during my recent trips to Normandy. My dreams have been following their normal course, meaning that I can see that my life continues normally in them. If a calamity were going to happen soon killing a third of the population, many people would already have had dreams of a very special kind[28] and in any case completely unrelated to our daily worries.

Carpe diem.

---

[28] In this work you will find examples of dreams by people approaching death: KELSEY Morton, Dreams*: A Way to Listen to God*, New York/Mahwah, Paulist Press, 1989.

REPLIES TO FREQUENT QUESTIONS

1: Why don't I dream?

It is recognised scientifically that everyone dreams, apart from those with serious brain injury. Dreaming is necessary for good physical and psychological health. It is quite easy for people who think they don't dream[29] to reactivate the memory of dreams. If you have problems in remembering your dreams, note down your impressions in the morning when awake, your emotional state. Do you feel sad, happy? Note down the thoughts that come to mind as soon as you open your eyes. Of course, if you wake up with a radio alarm clock which screams out "hello Simone", as this is not your name your brain will be immediately occupied in reflecting on the unexpected identity change. Likewise, if having hardly woken up, you mentally or physically rush into the day's activities, you will stand little chance of salvaging any scraps of dreams. Normally, all it takes is to be interested yourself in dreams in order to better remember them. Memory of dreams improves very quickly if it is called upon, and I have also noticed that simultaneously

---

[29] And who do not use medication which inhibits the ability to dream.

the memory of daily events is also improved. Conversely if you improve your memory in reality, that can only improve your memory of dreams. If you really cannot manage by any means to remember your dreams, you might think about using the training effect of other people who dream a lot and who remember their dreams. If you spend time with such people, that will help in relaunching your own 'oneiric mechanism'. Experiment with this. We communicate far more things than we think. However, before asking for outside help, make sure that you are sleeping enough. Indeed, if you are too tired and only sleep for the time strictly necessary for physical recovery, you will stand little chance of having a good memory for your dreams. If this is the case with you, try to prolong your sleeping time. Before going to sleep ask yourself to dream and remember your dreams. This works very well. You could also eat very lightly in the evening or change rooms. I have observed in the course of my research on the effects of crystals on the oneiric process and on sleep, that placing a beautiful quartz crystal point on the pillow has an amplifying effect on the memory of dreams. It also makes them clearer and brighter. It is an easy experiment to do and risk-free. Other methods have been suggested in works on dreams. Here are a few (that I haven't had need to test):

In a book on the yoga of dreams: it is advised to let more air and/or light into the place where you are sleeping, to visualise a red ball level with your throat chakra, or a white pearl on the forehead.[30]

In a book on lucid dreaming: it is advised to take a B6 supplement and to use nutmeg in your cooking. This book also advises the use of a cushion filled with mugwort (*artemesia vulgaris*) or the use of sage essential oil which has hypnotic properties. This oil must not be used if you have consumed alcohol, or at the same time as the cushion filled with mugwort. In addition, this cushion must not be used by pregnant women, because this plant contains a component which can cause a miscarriage.[31]

In a book on decoding dreams written by a psychologist [32] : we read that motivation is extremely important, that heavy and high fat foods, tobacco, alcohol and sedatives must be avoided. The author also points out the problem

---

[30] NORBU, NamKhai, *Le Yoga du Rêve*, *op. cit.*, p. 75.

[31] DEVEREUX Paul and DEVEREUX Charla, *The Lucid Dreaming Book, How to awake within, control and use your dreams, Boston, Tokio*, Journey Editions, 1998.

[32] SALVATGE Geneviève, *Décodez vos rêves*, Paris, Presses Pocket, 1992, p. 20-21 and 34-35.

with alarm clocks, which by waking you up suddenly, make you forget your dreams. To help, the book advises the glass of water method. This is what it consists of: in the evening you put a glass of water on your bedside table and before going to sleep drink a little bit, at the same time saying to yourself that tomorrow, when you drink the rest, you will remember your dreams. The author also mentions several floral elixirs that may help you, (blackberry, forget-me-not, orange tree, apple tree). She writes that the Deva Chaparral elixir helps with [33] the re-emergence of repressed emotions. She also mentions Dr. BACH's floral remedies. All these floral remedies, which are without side-effects, can be very useful. However, they are not absolutely necessary. You dream naturally and you can also remember your dreams naturally.

In a book on oneiric activity: it is advised to stay still, eyes closed when we wake up and to try to remember dreams. Changing the position of

---

[33] Laboratoires DEVA, P.P. 3, 38880 Autran; Dr Edward BACH Centre Mount Vernon, Wallingford, Oxon OX10-OPZ. In the United States, BACH flowers can be bought in health food shops. In the U.K they are very easy to find, in hardware stores, chemists and even in some airports. In France you can find them in health food shops and they are also sold in specialised shops such as Anthyllide, www.anthyllide.com.

your body in bed is then advised. Changing the position of the body often triggers the emergence of memories of dreams. This advice is given by Patricia GARFIELD in her book *Creative Dreaming*.[34]

In Hervey de Saint Denys's book on oneiric lucidity, a very astute method can be found to allow people to regain memory of their dreams, although it is quite hard to apply. I quote the author:

A close friend, with whom I went on a long trip and who was interested in my research, argued, convinced that he had never dreamt during quiet sleep. On many occasions I had woken him shortly after he had gone to sleep, and he had always assured me in very good faith that he couldn't remember any dreams. One night when he had been sleeping for about half an hour, I approached his bed; in a low voice I gave several military commands: Slope arms! Ready! etc., and I woke him gently.

"Well, did you not again this time?
- Nothing, absolutely nothing as far as I know.
- Search your mind thoroughly

---

[34] GARFIELD Patricia L., *La créativité onirique, Du rêve ordinaire au rêve lucide*, (original title: Creative Dreaming), Paris, J'ai Lu, 1974, p. 200.

- I'm really searching but can only find a period of absolute oblivion.
-Are you sure, I then asked, that you didn't even see a soldier?

At the mention of the word soldier he interrupted me as if struck by a sudden memory: "That's true! It's true! He said to me. Yes, I remember now; I dreamt I was present at a review. But how did you guess that?"

I asked permission to keep my secret until I had completed the experiment again. Close to him I whispered some horse riding terms and we had an almost identical conversation when he woke up. At first no notion of a dream came to mind; then, on my instructions he remembered many previous visions, which my intervention had disturbed.

A short while after this second experiment I did a third, which was just as successful. Instead of using words in order to influence my fellow traveller's dreams, I rang little bells lightly, the sound of which had given rise to the thought that we were continuing on our journey, in a mail coach which was travelling along the road.[35]

---

[35] Hervey de Saint Denys, *Les rêves et les Moyens de les Diriger, Observations pratiques*, Complete edition, Buenos Books International, Paris, p. 121.

2: How can I interpret my dreams?

At the start of the experiment simply take notes on your dreams and reality in the manner recommended in this book. Don't try to interpret your dreams immediately, you will understand them a lot more easily after a while, because as a result of doing this simple neutral observation work, you will automatically improve communication between your subconscious, your body and your conscious mind. This will lead to an improvement in the circulation of energy in your body. After some time[36], when you have collected together enough observations, all it will take is to reread all your information in one go. You will then see that the same oneiric symbols appear in relation to the same reality and this will enable you to understand the exact meaning of your own oneiric symbols. For example when I was a student and working as a temp, dreams about losing shoes related to a rationally unexpected, anticipated end of my temporary assignments in reality. Whereas the dreams in which I saw myself wearing a magnificent hat, heralded jobs of a higher intellectual status. This phenomenon will allow you to understand most of your dreams, in a far more reliable way than all the other methods for interpreting dreams which are generally used.

---

[36] It generally takes a year for the least gifted people.

As you have most probably understood, the dreamer's environment is a major factor in the content of dreams. Accordingly, in order to interpret them correctly, a simple account of a dream or series of dreams without knowing the context and the dreamer's habits, is not enough. To illustrate the difficulty of interpreting dreams without having information on the sleeper's reality, I am going to talk about the following dream taken from my dream notebook and which, despite my experience, I couldn't understand when I noted it down, but only after gathering some elements of the surrounding reality. It is as follows:

"Last night I had an amusing dream. I was in a really green park and the plants had lots of flowers in the form of cubes. There were cubes of all colours. I was very surprised that nature was able to produce this kind of flower in the form of cubes, which I had never seen before, and amused, I regarded the scene."

Should this dream be interpreted? I didn't try it myself, I knew that I would receive a reply otherwise. Indeed, after noting down this dream, I felt a strong need to go to the gardens of the Cité Internationale. And what a surprise I had there! In the garden a very original art exhibition had been organised; "presents" of all colours in the form of cubes had been displayed in the park. There was the reply I was looking for. My inexplicable dream was simply informing me of what was happening in my immediate environment, as I live close to the Cité Internationale. But by passing from my subconscious to my conscious through the channel of dreams, the information gathered in my environment had been 'organised' slightly to 'adapt' to my mind: the cardboard presents of all colours were transformed into blooming flowers on plants.

The message in dreams has often been transformed in relation to the reality that was captured subconsciously. For example if in dreams you receive information about somebody you don't yet know, in your dreams this person will often have the appearance of another person you already know and with whom he shares common features. Fortunately there are also many clear dreams which don't need interpretation. For example you might dream about a question that a colleague in the office asks you and this person will actually ask you this same question the day after or a week later. This kind of dream is extremely common.

After about a year observing your dreams and reality, you will have managed to interpret 90% of your oneiric symbols in a reliable and precise way. You will then understand how useless dream dictionaries are. Indeed everyone has their own oneiric language that is personal to them and which is a result of the way in which their brain was programmed in the first years of their lives.

Only in-depth personal work will allow you to interpret your own oneiric code, which will allow you to make effective use of your ability to dream. You will see that throughout your life your oneiric symbols remain relatively stable. This means that you learn all your oneiric language in the first years of your work. From time to time you will later learn other new symbolic meanings when new symbols relating to real new situations appear. This can be compared to learning your mother tongue. We learn this mostly in our first years.

If a new oneiric theme appears in your dreams and you do not want to wait to know the meaning of these dreams, you can help yourself by using all the advice that has been given by many authors, most of them psychologists, in order to interpret your dreams. For example you could use Gale Delaney's interview technique.[37] Robert Moss suggests re-entering dreams and reliving them.[38]

I stress again, above all do not rely on dream dictionaries or other dream keys to help you; they will only mislead and worry you. They are often full of superstitions and may sometimes be very negative. I have also noticed during the training that I give, that people who had been in the habit

---

[37] *Cf.* p. 38, on Gale Delaney's interview technique.
[38] Moss Robert, *Dreamsgate*, op. cit., p. 42.

of using a dream interpretation dictionary for many years had programmed their dreams and their brain to dream in accordance with the content of their dictionary. By doing so they drastically limited their access to the information field which opens naturally when we observe our dreams and reality with all the neutrality of a researcher.

Instead of using dream keys, on the contrary think about understanding your dreams in relation to the processes at work in nature. Through my research I have been able to observe that the subconscious is closely linked to nature, that most of the time it speaks 'nature's language' and many symbols can be understood with reference to nature and how it works. For example, in a dream, a plant that is growing signifies the growth of something in your psyche or sometimes in your wallet or in your feelings. Water that gives life is often a synonym for energy and leaks show the dreamer his energetic leaks, etc.

From this point of view a symbols dictionary is a good tool to work with. In French you can use the *Dictionnaire des Symboles* by Jean Chevalier and Alain Gheerbrant.[39]

---

[39] For example: Chevalier Jean, Gheerbrant Alain, *Dictionnaire des Symboles*, Laffont, Jupiter, collection Bouquins, Paris, 1982.

Finally, when you wish to interpret your dreams, listen to your intuition and really pay attention to emotions felt in the dream. They are key in understanding the meaning of dreams. For me personally, it is mainly intuition that guides me when someone asks me to interpret a dream. Sometimes I intuitively have an immediate answer; other times my intuition asks me appropriate questions about the dreamer's environment. Sometimes I have the intuition that this dream does not concern the person who is describing it. Also sometimes I dream about the dream that is going to be described to me and its interpretation, before meeting the people who in reality will tell me their dreams. Often on holiday, on a train or plane, in a park or restaurant, I meet a stranger who doesn't normally pay any attention to his dreams but will feel an irrepressible need to tell me a dream that has really affected him, and ask me what I think about it, even though he doesn't know that I am so interested in dreams! In these cases, for the person concerned it relates to a very important message that his subconscious wanted to communicate with to him. But not being able to do this directly, it organised in the world of dreams this meeting, which in reality seems to have happened "by pure chance".

3: Through dreams can we receive information from distant places and people?

The answer is: yes. But I cannot give you a scientific explanation for this phenomenon, which is however natural and common. I have noticed throughout my research that my body was able to receive information from people far away. While I was in Paris I dreamt of precise information concerning an event that was happening in China near Shanghai and which concerned a dear Chinese friend. I regularly dream of information concerning a friend who lives in New York which I can check with her by telephone or email.

I also regularly 'project myself in dreams' to unknown places that I have to go to. I pick up information concerning these places and the people who live there, before going. My dreams thereby make my travels a lot easier and warn me of potential dangers.

I have noticed that I don't pick up information about things that don't interest me and that don't have any psychological affinity with me. In dreams geographical distance is no impediment for access to information. What prevails then is the law of attraction, affinities and interests.

In dreams the law of attraction by affinity (what belongs together comes together) plays a major role in receiving information from distant places and people. However, while you receive information from very far away people or places, your immediate environment and your own information sphere will "colour" and sometimes deform the information that you receive from a distance. Some kinds of information and energies will be drawn in by you according to your interests, your energy level and also the objects that surround you where you are sleeping. If, for example, you sleep with an object near you that belongs to someone who is close to you who is away, it is highly probable that you will pick up information concerning this person because you are sleeping with an object near you that belongs to them, which is therefore full of their energetic information. I very often dream of people who read my books on dreams and I talk to them about this.

Many spiritual traditions have mentioned the fact that when we sleep we can leave our body, travel, meet people and sort out problems, etc. You will see yourself through observation of the oneiric process that it is a common phenomenon. When this phenomenon occurs, you will notice that although you are outside your body, it continues actively to pick up information that you continue to receive as if you were in your body and outside of it at the same time.

It is also possible to leave your body upon waking by using particular techniques. There are very interesting books where methods for leaving your own body voluntarily upon waking are explained. Some authors believe that these practices are risk-free, but not all authors believe this. I find all this research on leaving your body upon waking fascinating, but personally I prefer to leave my own body (sometimes called astral voyages) during dreams, because this is done naturally, when we have the right level of energy and are calm enough to do this, and it is without risk.

BIBLIOGRAPHY

Recent works on dreams:

Shamanic approaches:

MOSS Robert, Dreaming True, *How to Dream Your Future and Change Your Life for the Better*, New York, Pocket Books, 2000.

www.mossdreams.com

MAGAÑA Sergio, *The Dawn of the Sixth Sun*, Edizioni Amrita SRL, 2012

This Mexican shaman teaches the art of dreaming according to the tradition of the ancient Mexicans

www.concienciadimensional.com/en/members.html

Yogic approach:

NORBU NamKhai, *Dream Yoga and the Practice of Natural Light*, New York, Snow Lion Publications, 1992. (French translation Le *Yoga du Rêve*, Paris, J.L. Accarias, 1993, collection L'originel, translation by arrangement with Snow

Lion Publications, Ithaca, New York 14851, Editor KATZ, Michel translation by GAUDEBERT Gisèle).(Yoga approach)

In the dream tantra, the aim is preparation for the passage of death. This approach advises against dwelling on the analysis of dreams and phenomena such as telepathy or knowledge of the future which happen during dreams. She states that the development of the consciousness leads to total suppression of dreams.

Psychological approach:

DELANEY Gale, *All About Dreams, Everything You Need to Know About Why We Have Them, What They Mean, and How To Put Them to Work for You*, New York, HarperCollins, Harper Sanfrancisco, 1988

Open psychological approach to dreams. It is a very complete work, which is a list of all the theories on dreams since antiquity and throughout the world. This exhaustive and critical study on the history of the psychoanalytical approach to dreams is very interesting.

SALVATGE Geneviève, *Décodez vos rêves*, Paris, Presses Pocket, 1992

Religious approach to dreams:

KELSEY Morton, *Dreams: A Way to Listen to God,* New York/Mahwah, Paulist Press, 1989

This book written by an open-minded pastor is very interesting due to the critique of the Christian church's attitude throughout history on dreams. It is also very interesting for its examples of dreams that warn of death.

Approach using dream control techniques, lucid dreams:

LABERGE Stephen and RHEINGOLD Howard, *Exploring the World of Lucid Dreaming*, New York, Ballantine Books, 1992.

LABERGE Stephen, *Lucid Dreaming*, Ballantine Books, 1990.

DEVEREUX Paul and DEVEREUX Charla, *The Lucid Dreaming Book, How to awake within, control and use your dreams*, Boston, Tokio, Journey Editions, 1998.

CASTANEDA Carlos, *The Art of Dreaming*, William Morrow Paperbacks, 1994.

This author is very famous, but his books aren't always easy to understand, not to mention that the important information is drowned in a great quantity of text. We can benefit from reading the following author who has written an excellent synthesis of the most important information on the art of dreaming, contained in Castaneda's oeuvre: *The Teachings of Don Carlos: Practical Applications of the Works of Carlos Castaneda*, Victor Sanchez, Bear and Company, 1995

<u>Scientific, biological approach to dreams:</u>

See the University of Lyon's website 1: http://sommeil.univ-lyon1.fr/index_f.html

JOUVET Michel, *Le sommeil et le rêve*, Paris, O. Jacob, 2000.

WOODS Ralph L. and GREENHOUSE Herbert B., Editors, *The New World of Dreams*, New York, Macmillan Publishing Co, inc., 1974.

In this book you will find many articles written by scientists who have studied sleep, its cycles, the effects of drugs, medicines, alcohol and stimulants on the oneiric process, the effects of sleep deprivation on man and animals, or REM sleep cycle deprivation.

<u>For a synthesis of the many approaches to dreams:</u>

GARFIELD Patricia L., *Creative Dreaming*, Touchstone, 1995

COXHEAD David et HILLER Susan, *Dreams, Visions of the Night*, Thames and Hudson, 1989

Ancient authors and "classic" litterature on dreams:

ARISTOTLE, *La Vérité des songes, De la divination dans le sommeil*, (Parva Naturalia 462 b - 464 b), translated from the Greek and presented by Jackie Pigeaud, Paris, Rivages Poche, 1995

E. R. DODDS, *Les Grecs et l'irrationnel*, Paris, Aubier, 1965. "Supernormal phenomena in Classical Antiquity", in *The Ancient Concept of Progress and other Essays on Greek Literature and Belief*, Clarendon Press, Oxford, 1973

ARTEMIDORUS, *The Interpretation of Dreams: Oneirocritica*, Translated by R. J. White, Park Ridge, N.J., Noyes Press, 1975

FREUD Sigmund, *The Interpretation of Dreams*, New York: Avon Books, 1965 (first publication in 1900) (psychology)

JUNG Carl Gustav, *Memories, Dreams and Reflections*, London, Routledge and Kegan paul, 1963 (psychology)

D'HERVEY DE SAINT-DENYS, Marie Jean Léon (1822-1892: a precursor in this field), *Les rêves et les moyens de les diriger*, Buenos Books International, 2008. This book contains the author's observations on his own experiences of oneiric lucidity.

SAINT-DENIS H., *Dreams and How to Guide Them*, London, Duckworth, 1982. (Lucid dreaming), this book is very hard to find, and is not a complete translation of Saint-Denys's Work.

Works on scientific experiments aimed at proving the existence of telepathy in dreams, in a hypnotic state and during wakefulness

WOODS Ralph L. and GREENHOUSE Herbert B., Editors, *The New World of Dreams*, New York, Macmillan Publishing Co, inc., second printing 1974, p. 273 et seq. et p. 405 et seq.

DOSSEY, Larry, *Reinventing Medicine: Beyond Mind-Body To A New Era Of Healing*, New York, Harper Collins, 1999 in the first chapters gives an account of all the scientific experiments carried out in the United States, sometimes by prestigious institutions such as Harvard University, in Boston.

FERGUSON, Marilyn, *La révolution du cerveau*, Paris, J'ai Lu, 1973, original title: The Brain Revolution.

ABOUT THE COVER ILLUSTRATOR

Cristiane Mancini, the author's cousin, was born and lives in Brazil, Sao Paulo, where she is an illustrator. An artist at heart and talented, she likes illustrating all kinds of books, designing book covers, and also creating logos and other advertising designs.

She has already illustrated many books and amongst them children's books such as: "Fada Helena Boazinha" (Karen Vogel Camargo/

Publisher Núcleo Paradigma) and “A ilha encantada das Marias sem vergonha/ Busy lizzy´s enchanted island”. (Manuela Viera do Amaral/ Publisher Panamby Bilingual School See Saw).

Contact: mancinicristiane@yahoo.com.br

ABOUT THE TRANSLATOR

James Greenfield is a professional translator from Worcester, UK, who prides himself on delivering fluent and accurate translations from French to English and Spanish to English. His experience includes non-fiction translation and work for agencies and private clients on legal, financial and business texts.

Contact: greenfield.james@yahoo.co.uk

Other Books in English by Anna Mancini

ISBN: 9781932848434

The Meaning of Dreams

Dreams are at the heart of a process where tangible and intangible worlds are intimately intermingled. Indeed, a dream is an intangible phenomenon occurring in a physical body that stands in an environment both material and informational (intangible). A systematic investigation of the connections between dreams and reality sheds new light on the dream process and on the functioning of the mind. This book invites you, the reader, to discover the results you can achieve through a more comprehensive and unified approach to the dream process. It gives you advice on how to carry out your own research. Reading this book will help you become better aware of the role played by your body at the meeting point between dreams and reality, between the tangible and the intangible (Chapter 1). The book describes an efficient method for observing the dream process (Chapter 2) and explains the results you can achieve with it through your own experimentation (Chapter 3). Through your personal exploration of the whole dream process you will be able to verify for yourself the reality of certain faculties of the mind which are commonly considered to be "paranormal". You will see that they can be explained rationally. Chapter 4 of the book explains how you can use the dream process to find answers to your questions, whether they regard your daily life (health, work, relationships, life guidance) or your artistic or scientific creativity. The last chapter (Chapter 5) explains why faculties today considered to be paranormal are destined to a natural collective awakening.With this book, I invite you to observe your dreams and their connections with your reality, with a mind as neutral as possible. This is the best way to understand the meaning of your dreams. Try, then, to forget all you have ever heard about dreams, and just look at them and observe the whole dream process, and not only the dreams. Everything I assert in the book can be verified through personal experience by using the proposed method of observation. With this method everyone, even the most skeptical person, can verify the existence of unusual faculties of the mind, and learn to develop and use them.Key words: dreams and reality, precognitive dreams, future in dreams, premonitory dreams, dream interpretation, meaning of dreams, paranormal faculties, telepathy, dreams and health, dreams and abundance, dreams and the past, mind and body, nightmares, dreaming brain, lucid dreams

ISBN: 978193284804

Ancient Roman Solutions to Modern Legal Issues, the Example of Patent Law

Our Law and its philosophy have been conceived for an economic world where the main source of wealthwas material. Although this world no longer exists, its laws are still alive and slow down the developmentof modern economies. Patent law strikingly shows this fact. Invented mainly during the industrial revolutionin order to protect tangible inventions, it could not be applied to the new intangible inventions of the 20th century. Software, for example, has been denied protection under patent law, due to its lack of materiality. Since such a cause of denial is economically absurd, we should adapt patent law to the virtual world. Thiswas not done and so no new intangible invention can benefit from this protection through a lack of tangibility.Long before us, the ancient Romans had understood that the intangible world and the material world do not function the same way. Since they were very practical people, they took this reality into account to buildtheir legal system. Their legal experience has become valuable for a modern world that is rediscovering thevalue of ideas and people's wealth, too long eclipsed by materialism.

ISBN: 9781932848106

Maat Revealed, Philosophy of Justice in Ancient Egypt

Unlike ancient Rome, Egypt did not transmit any legal system to us, but rather an idea of justice our modern mindscan hardly understand. In the ancient Egyptian world, almost all the texts and inscriptions speak of justice. All thetexts of wisdom teach that one has to conform to Maat, an obscure and omnipresent concept that Egyptologists havetranslated into the expression "Goddess of Truth and Justice".Egyptian justice is so different from ours that Egyptologists and historians of religions believe they have not yet fullyunderstood its meaning. They regret this fact because understanding Maat would be a gateway to a deeper understanding of the ancient Egyptian world. As for lawyers, they have limited themselves to the Greco-Roman sources on the philosophy of Justice and the discoveries of Egyptologists in this philosophical field remain thoroughly ignored. Thanks to her experience in ancient history of law and her ability to understand ancient symbols, the author provides Egyptologywith the missing pieces that were needed to form a coherent image of Maat. Once revealed, Maat sheds a new and unexpected light on the whole of Egyptian civilization. As a bridge between traditionally separate fields of academicresearch, this book is a useful and groundbreaking contribution to Egyptology, the history of religions and the modernphilosophy of law.

ISBN: 9781932848328

How to unlock the secrets, enigmas and mysteries of Ancient Egypt and other old civilizations

I realized while I was researching Maat, the ancient goddess of justice, how hard it was for Egyptologists to understand most of the ancient Egyptian artifacts only with their conscious mind. Our modern mental structure bars us from entering and comprehending the logic of ancient peoples. The difference in understanding the world is why so many aspects of ancient cultures remain enigmaticand strange, even for the most intelligent modern scholars. The ancient people possessed a much bettersense of the energies of life and nature than modern man does. These ancients explored the laws and properties of the intangible world and its action upon the material world. They gained valuable knowledgethat has been preserved in their archeological remains as well as in their archaic legal systems. This typeof knowledge was often rendered in symbolic dream-like language and images that modern scholars arenot trained to understand. Moreover, even when this knowledge is rendered in remarkably clear language,how can one fully understand what one has never experienced? It is when we dream that we come closer to the mental universe of ancient peoples. While dreaming,modern man becomes like the ancients-aware and concerned about life-energy, a capacity modernman has now lost in his waking state. Through learning a unique technique to decipher their dreams, modern scholars would be enabled to understand more fully and perfectly how ancient people perceivedthe world around them differently.In this book, you will find an explanation of the technique I teach in my workshops, which is based on more than 20 years of personal research of ancient legal systems and the connections betweendreams and reality. My approach is completely different from and much more practical than other techniques regarding dreams. This teaching would be of great help and benefit to all scholars an intelligentpeople who endeavor to advance our understanding of the ancient Egyptian civilization and of other ancient worlds.

ISBN: 9781932848243

Scientific Creativity, Useful Information for Students and Research Teams

Throughout history famous researchers had innovative dreams that sometimes won them a Nobel Prize. Why did they have these dreams? Based on 20 years innovative work on the connections between dreamsand reality and on the role played by the whole body in the innovative dream process, this revolutionary book answers many questions about scientific creativity and how to boost it. It explains why innovative dreams, ideas and intuitions occur and what blocks them. It reveals how researchers can place themselvesin the best conditions to become discoverers. It teaches a powerful technique to provoke innovative dreams,ideas and intuitions instead of waiting for the stroke of luck.

ISBN: 9781932848182

Copyright Law Is Obsolete

Copyright laws worldwide were created for a publishing world where books were tangible, printed in a limited number and sold within territory based markets. Technological changes are giving place to a new book market where books are intangible, exist in unlimited number of copies and travel worldwide in an increasingly global market. In this emerging global book market made possible by the conjunction of the Internet, e-book technologies, DRM and print on demand devices, the three important legal concepts traditionally used in copyright laws have become obsolete: territory, property and the Aristotelian idea of justice. These three concepts were well suited to the tangible book market but are no longer for the virtual book market where persons matter more than objects. This book invites the reader to explore the specific functioning of the virtual economy. It proposes guidelines to modernize copyright law so that it can foster an adequate use of new communication technologies. For the first time in History, the humankind has acquired a technology that allows to create a world of information affluence and freedom of speech or its opposite.This book explains why the option for abundance and freedom must prevail, how the law can support this movementand what would be, to the contrary, the disastrous consequences of the other option. This book goes beyond a simple reflection on the book market and considers the choice of society, even of civilization implied by the use, right or wrong, of the new communication technologies.

ISBN: 9781932848175

International Patent Law Is Obsolete

Since it was developed mainly during the industrial revolution to protect material innovations, patent law cannot be applied to "intangible industrial inventions". Software for example is denied patentability dueto its lack of materiality. Such a justification for this denial is economic nonsense, international patent lawmust be adapted to cover the emerging virtual world. This has not been done. Unsuited to modern innovation, international patent law has reached a period of decline. This decline is due to the fact thatdespite the existence of international agreements, States have now come to ignore the framework of thepatent system (for software) and sometimes to adopt new international agreements (for semi-conductor chips). This book explains how we reached this situation, and how and why we should urgently modernizeand rebalance the international patent system. Publisher's note: This book is an abridged version of the out print book: Proposals for a worldwide changeof Patent law, published by Innovative Justice in 1994. It does not list all the case law now available on theissue of computer software. This can now be found in digital databases and no longer needs to be printed. This book brings thoughts that are still new in the legal establishement and points out how we could improvethe international patent system.

ISBN: 9781932848083

Internet Justice, Philosophy of Law for the Virtual World

Our law and its philosophy were conceived for a material economic world marked by scarcity and territoriality. Without the criterion of territoriality, the dominant philosophies of law are left bankrupt. This is especially thecase for KELSEN's Pure Theory of Law, in which the territoriality criterion is the cornerstone. Since the world of Internet is marked by abundance rather than scarcity, it has no territorial boundaries and it is not material, it is easy to understand that it cannot be efficientlymanaged according to our traditional legaland philosophical principles. On the Internet, even the Aristotelian concept of justice -which gives each his own and shares a limited amount of goods- is old hat. Although our law only recognizes this concept of justice and its nuances - as in RAWLS' Theory of Justice-, it is however impossible to apply this idea of justice efficiently in cyberspace. This book proposes a philosophy of justice suited to the virtual world and some legal principles that law-makerscould apply to act efficiently and help the development of the Internet and the Information Society.

www.ingramcontent.com/pod-product-compliance
Lightning Source LLC
Chambersburg PA
CBHW060400090426
42734CB00011B/2207